OEDIPUS AND THE OEDIPUS COMPLEX

OEDIPUS AND THE OEDIPUS COMPLEX

A Revision

Siegfried Zepf, Florian Daniel Zepf, Burkhard Ullrich, and Dietmar Seel

KARNAC

Originally published in Germany as *Ödipus und der Ödipuskomplex. Eine Revision* by Siegfried Zepf, Florian Daniel Zepf, Burkhard Ullrich, Dietmar Seel

First published in English in 2017 by
Karnac Books Ltd
118 Finchley Road
London NW3 5HT

British Library Cataloguing in Publication Data

A C.I.P. for this book is available from the British Library

ISBN-13: 978-1-78220-419-0

Typeset by Medlar Publishing Solutions Pvt Ltd, India

Printed in Great Britain

www.karnacbooks.com

CONTENTS

ACKNOWLEDGEMENTS

We would like to thank Simon Thomas and Judith Zepf for their pains-taking work in editing the original manuscript.

We are also indebted to the following publishers/copyright-holders for their kind permission to cite from these works in our book:

John Wiley & Sons for permission to cite from "The origins and development of the Oedipus complex" by Serge Lebovici (Presented at the 32nd International Psychoanalytical Congress, Helsinki, July 1981; Copyright© Serge Lebovici); for permission to cite from "Specific forms of the Oedipus complex" by Otto Fenichel; for permission to cite from "Turning a blind eye: The cover up for Oedipus" by John Steiner (Copyright© John Steiner).

Brandes & Apsel Verlag for permission to cite from "Von der eingeschränkten zur allgemeinen Verführungstheorie" by Jean Laplanche.

Stanford University Press for permission to cite from *Dialectic of Enlightenment* by Max Horkheimer and Theodor W. Adorno.

ABOUT THE AUTHORS

Dietmar Seel, Dipl.—Psych., since 2000 a practising psychoanalyst in Saarbrücken (Germany). Former scientific assistant at the Institute of Psychoanalysis, Psychotherapy and Psychosomatic Medicine of the University Clinics of the Saarland. Member of the Saarland Institute for Psychoanalysis and Psychotherapy and of the DGPT.

Burkhard Ullrich, Dipl.—Psych., since 2000 a practising psychoanalyst in Neunkirchen (Germany). Former scientific assistant at the Institute of Clinic Psychology of the University of the Saarland (Germany), at the Research Institute for Psychotherapy in Stuttgart (Germany) and at the Institute of Psychoanalysis, Psychotherapy and Psychosomatic Medicine of the University Clinics of the Saarland. Member of the Saarland Institute of Psychoanalysis and Psychotherapy and of the DGPT.

Florian Daniel Zepf, Prof. M. D., Chair and Winthrop Professor of Child and Adolescent Psychiatry at the University of Western Australia in Perth, Clinical Director/Head of Department of the Specialised Child and Adolescent Mental Health Services in Western Australia. Numerous publications in the field of child and adolescent psychiatry and psychotherapy.

x   ABOUT THE AUTHORS

Siegfried Zepf, Univ.—Prof. em. M. D., 1992–2002 director of the Institute of Psychoanalysis, Psychotherapy and Psychosomatic Medicine of the University Clinics of the Saarland (Germany). Training analyst (DPG, DGPT), numerous book publications and publications in scientific journals (see the homepage of the Saarland Institute for Psychoanalysis and Psychotherapy [http://www.sipp.de/index.php?id=63 last accessed 21 April 2016]).

INTRODUCTION

When one reads or hears about Freud's Oedipus complex nowadays everything appears to be quite straightforward. The Oedipus complex is understood as the "*nuclear complex of every neurosis*" (Freud, 1910a, p. 47) originating in the "archaic heritage" of mankind (1939a, p. 99) and is thus regarded as ubiquitous—"Every new arrival on this planet is faced by the task of mastering the Oedipus complex; anyone who fails to do so falls a victim to neurosis" (1905d, p. 226). In the heterosexual version of this complex, the son loves and desires his mother and wants to eliminate his father; the daughter loves and desires her father and wants to get rid of her mother. In the homosexual edition, the son loves and desires his father and wants to do away with his mother; the daughter loves and desires her mother and wants to get rid of her father.

However, the assumed clarity proves to be nebulous on several grounds. Remembering that in "jest—it is well known—one may even tell the truth" (Freud, 1915b, p. 298), one might for instance recall a well-known Jewish joke—a son coming back from his first analytic session tells his Jewish mother that the analyst has diagnosed an Oedipus complex, and his mother says: "Oh, Oedipus, shmoedipus, you'll be all right as long as you love your mother!"—or bear in mind Federn's

xi

statement at a meeting of the Vienna Psychoanalytic Society in 1914: "Of importance also is the parent's behavior: it is Laius who exposes Oedipus" (Nunberg & Federn, 1975, p. 254) or be reminded of Freud's assertion that the "foundation for a neurosis would ... always be laid in childhood by adults" (1896c, pp. 207f.). If Freud's statements are taken seriously—the mother regards her child with "feelings that are derived from her own sexual life", treats her child "as a substitute for a complete sexual object" (1905d, p. 223), by "her care of the child's body she becomes his first seducer" (1940a, p. 65), and that the "affections of the little girl are fixed on her father, who has probably done all he could to win her love, and in this way has sown the seeds of an attitude of hatred and rivalry towards her mother" (1919e, p. 186)—and if one supports Fenichel's assertion that the "children's Oedipus complex reflects the parents unsolved Oedipus complex" (1945, p. 93), one is confronted with a completely different state of affairs. *The enlightenment of the Oedipus myth with the help of the Oedipus complex, which Freud claims for himself, appears itself to be a myth requiring enlightenment.*

For this purpose we will concentrate on the myths that Freud either neglected or understood as a manifestation of the Oedipus complex. That is to say, we go along with Edmunds (1985) in reversing the process of examining the relationship between the Oedipus complex and Oedipus myths in such a way that the myths are not interpreted in the light of the Oedipus complex but that the Oedipus myths can be put to use to analyse the Oedipus complex. In other words, an investigation of differing Oedipus myths may be able to provide information on aspects of the oedipal drama that were not adequately addressed by Freud.

Since the myths focus primarily on the male oedipal drama, this will also be in the nucleus of our considerations without neglecting the female drama totally. We will begin by giving a short sketch of Sophocles' *Oedipus Tyrannus* focusing in particular on those aspects which Freud did not take notice of, we will query whether Freud was justified in excluding these aspects, and if that does not prove to be the case, give attention to insights that may be inherent in the excluded aspects so as to gain a deeper understanding of the Oedipus complex.

Our investigation is confronted with a variety of elaborations of the oedipal theme, all of which can scarcely be examined in one paper. A few of the authors of such elaborations include Euripides and Aeschylus (Christ, 1905), Achaios, Theodectes, Xenocles, Carcinas and Diogenes (Nauck, 1889), and Seneca, Julius Caesar, Corneille, Voltaire, Hölderlin,

Hugo von Hofmannsthal (Rank, 1926, p. 191ff.). Following this, we will restrict ourselves to those aspects of Sophocles' drama that Freud omitted and those that Devereux (1953) takes from Greek mythology. Furthermore, we will consider some mythological details concerning Oedipus, Jocasta, Laius, and Pelops with which, in all likelihood, Freud was familiar.

Before the Oedipus complex attained its central position in the aetiology of neuroses, seduction was assumed to be central. It was Kris who used the term "seduction theory" (Blass & Simon, 1994, p. 678) for Freud's assumption that neurosis can always be traced back to sexual seduction. Thus, we will present an outline of the so-called "seduction theory" and elucidate the question whether Freud's neglect of certain aspects of the Oedipus drama and his rejection of seduction theory have reasons in common. This is followed by a brief account of the Oedipus complex, the arguments Freud put forward to justify this complex phylogenetically, and his theory of the possible dissolution of this complex. Following this, we will pay attention to the Oedipus myths concerning Laius, Jocasta, and the Sphinx, and then discuss the psychological reasons that may have led Freud to discard the idea of parental neuroses for the development of the Oedipus complex. We will then confront Freud's Oedipus complex with the Oedipus myths, which decipher und expose the complex as a cover story. Finally, we will return to Sophocles' drama *Oedipus at Colonus*. Here Oedipus loses his blindness and Sophocles' reveals to us the veiled secrets that remain hidden to both Oedipus in *Oedipus Tyrannus* and to Freud. The process of de-mystification we have undertaken leads us finally to admit an entirely divergent conception of the Oedipus complex.

CHAPTER ONE

Two questions

> Myth is already enlightenment and enlightenment reverts to mythology.
>
> —Max Horkheimer and Theodor W. Adorno,
> 1944, p. XVIII

In his five lectures on psychoanalysis published in 1910, Freud emphasises for the first time that the Oedipus complex is the *"nuclear complex of every neurosis"* (Freud, 1910a, p. 47). Two years later he sees the Oedipus complex as part of mankind's heritage (1912–1913a, p. 160, pp. 141f.).

It is well known that Freud borrowed the name for this complex from Sophocles' drama *Oedipus Tyrannus* with which he had been familiar since 1873 (letter to Emil Fluss, 16 June 1873, 1960a, p. 4). As a reminder: Oedipus frees Thebes from the Sphinx by solving her riddle, becomes the widowed Queen Jocasta as his wife and thereby becomes King, visits Thebes to discover the cause of the plague threatening Thebes. Oedipus sends his brother-in-law Creon to the oracle at Delphi to find out how he might save Thebes from the plague. Creon returns with the message that Thebes can only be spared from the disease if the murderer of the former King Laius is found and expelled from the country.

On his search for Laius' murderer Oedipus calls for the blind seer Teiresias and questions him to reveal the truth. Teiresias avoids replying, whereupon Oedipus accuses him of being in league with Creon in planning and executing the murder of Laius. This accusation infuriates Teiresias, who promptly accuses Oedipus of being Laius' murderer and of taking Laius' wife, his own mother, to be his wife and of fathering children with her.

Creon hears of Oedipus' accusation and the two argue violently. Jocasta, Oedipus' wife and Creon's sister, intervenes. She reveals to Oedipus that before the birth of her son an oracle prophesied that this child would kill his father Laius. Three days after the birth Laius accordingly pierced their son's ankles and abandoned him in the mountains. Many years later, Laius was killed at a place where three roads meet.

Jocasta's confession sets Oedipus thinking. He says he did hear a rumour that he was not the biological son of the parents he grew up with and to dispel his doubts he had visited the oracle. The oracle had proclaimed that he would kill his father and marry his mother. Fearing that he might harm his parents he had left the country. On his way he had killed a man and one of his companions at a place where three roads meet. The other man fled.

Jocasta mentions that the servant who had fled had asked to be dismissed as soon as he learned that Oedipus was to become king. To clarify this Oedipus decides to talk to this servant. But before he can do this a messenger arrives from Corinth and reports that Polybus, Oedipus' stepfather, has died, but of natural causes. Oedipus now has hopes that he has not killed his father. However, when shortly afterwards a further messenger reports that after having received the infant Oedipus from one of Laius' men he brought him to Polybus, Oedipus' hope is finally shattered.

It turns out that the man who rescued Oedipus is the servant Oedipus sought after. Under threat of torture this man confirms Oedipus' fears saying that he had orders to kill Oedipus, but that he did not have the heart to do so. Instead he delivered Oedipus into the care of the messenger from Corinth.

Oedipus' guilt can no longer be denied. Jocasta returns to the palace and shortly afterwards a servant comes out, reporting that Jocasta has hanged herself after hearing the news that Oedipus was none other than her son. Oedipus blinds himself by stabbing his eyes out, admits his guilt publicly, and pleads to Creon, now king, to banish him from the country and to take care of his children.

The universality of the Oedipus complex has been subjected to much critical discussion (e.g., Basch, 1986; Fenichel, 1930; Parin, 1977) and its phylogenetic justification has been questioned with strong arguments (e.g., Mitchell, 1982; Moore & Fine, 1990, p. 147; Zepf & Zepf, 2011). However, with few exceptions, among them Adler, Devereux, Fromm, Horney, Jung, Rank, and Ross (see, Galdstone, 1976, p. 260), Freud's understanding of the complex that the son competes with his father for his mother and wants to eliminate him as his rival, the daughter competes with her mother for her father and wants to do away with her, has remained basically unchanged in psychoanalysis (see, e.g., Fitzpatrick-Hanly, 2007; Laine, 2007; Reed, 2008).

This is surprising because in his reasoning, Freud refers not just to the name but also to the Greek mythology as shown in Sophocles' drama and, although he must have been familiar with this drama—in the letter we have cited Freud writes that the "Greek paper, consisting of a thirty-three-verse passage from Oedipus Rex ... I had also read on my own account" (letter to Emil Fluss, 16 June 1873, 1960a, p. 4)—, he nonetheless ignores certain aspects portrayed in the myths. For instance, at the 8 April 1914 meeting of the Vienna Psychoanalytic Society, Federn states, "Of importance also is the parent's behavior: it is Laius who exposes Oedipus" (Nunberg & Federn, 1975, p. 254). Although Freud (1900a, p. 261) mentions the reasons for Oedipus' exposure to this treatment as an infant, he did not discuss the cruelty of the parents (Schneiderhan, 1852, p. 25) associated with it or comment on the piercing of Oedipus' ankles.[1] The same holds true for the supposition arising in Sophocles' play that Jocasta probably knew the true identity of Oedipus, Stewart (1961) for instance, in consideration of the difference in the degrees of punishment for Jocasta and Oedipus, concludes that Jocasta commits her crimes knowingly, but Oedipus' actions are not premeditated. Jocasta only commits the crime of incest and her punishment is suicide, whereas Oedipus is guilty of committing the crimes of both incest and parricide but his punishment is only self-blinding and banishment from Thebes. Blanck (1984), Bross (1984) and Naiman (1992) substantiate the idea that Jocasta co-staged the drama by pointing to the following aspects:

- Jocasta lies to Oedipus when she tells him that it was Laius alone who gave her son away

- she tells Oedipus that his appearance is similar to that of Laius
- she tries in vain to persuade Oedipus to abandon his quest for the death of Laius
- she informs Oedipus that her son's ankles were pinioned when Laius gave him away and the scars resulting from this pinioning were visible when Jocasta first met Oedipus as an adult.

Robert (1915, p. 62) argues that the pierced ankles have no practical relevance and are only introduced in the drama as a means of recognition.[2] It was illogical to assume that Oedipus' ankles were pierced to contribute to the death of the child because the child could have easily been killed at any time. It was also absurd to assume that this piercing was intended to prevent the escape of a three-day-old infant (Roscher, 1897–1909, p. 705).

Furthermore, when Jocasta consoles Oedipus that in their dreams many men make love to their mothers, but they go about their life without being troubled by the idea,[3] Freud neglects looking at the relevance of this for her relationship with Oedipus. He overlooks the fact that Jocasta talks about the oracle Laius has received without mentioning the prophesied incest—she only states "χρησμὸς γὰρ ἦλθε Λαΐῳ ποτ', οὐκ ἐρῶ ... ὡς αὐτὸν ἥξοι μοῖρα πρὸς παιδὸς θανεῖν ὅστις γένοιτ' ἐμοῦ τε κἀκείνου πάρα" (Sophocles, 1991, 711–714)[4]—and the fact that she commits suicide immediately after the incest comes to light (ibid., 1068). In contrast, Oedipus refers to the oracle always starting with the incest and continuing with the prophesied murder of his father (ibid., 791, 826, 976, 995; see also Halter, 1998, p. 44).

These omissions are worthy of notice. In Freud's (1925d, p. 69) view, myths are "imaginative creations of groups and peoples". They have latent content (1901a, p. 685; 1910a, p. 36) which always has to be uncovered (e.g., 1908e, p. 152; 1910a, p. 36; 1924f, p. 208; 1932a, p. 187) and it is surprising that Freud, despite these general views, subscribes to Sophocles' presentation and even scotomises aspects of the drama.

Additionally, Freud does not take note of a further myth in which Jocasta receives milder punishment than Oedipus. In this myth, Jocasta is thought of in the underworld after her death as having married her son after he murdered his father. The gods discover the incest instantly, Jocasta commits suicide and although Oedipus is persecuted by the Erinyes of his mother, he still remains King of Thebes and after his death in battle he is buried with heroic honours (Preller, 1875, p. 344; Roscher, 1897–1909, p. 701; St. Clair, 1961).

Freud does not consider the differing configurations of the oedipal drama in Greek mythology. Most of these configurations are mentioned in Roscher's *Lexikon der griechischen und römischen Mythologie*, in Preller's *Griechische Mythologie*—Freud quotes both sources in his writings (e.g., Freud, 1901b, p. 218; 1910c, p. 88; 1913f, p. 298)—and in Constans' (1881) *Le Légende d'Œdipe*.[5] Freud had this book in his library and marked several passages in this work, particularly those which had to do with incest (Roll & Abel, 1988).

In the light of this one may wonder why Freud saw no need to question Sophocles' drama *Oedipus Tyrannus* and to look for the latent content in the myths, despite his view that myths are more or less disguised conscious manifestations of unconscious contents (e.g., Freud, 1910a, p. 36). Possibly Freud believed he had already discovered the latent content of Sophocles' *Oedipus Tyrannus*, this being the Oedipus complex, so that he had no further interest in this issue. Assuming this, it is understandable why subsequent psychoanalysts have focused their investigations of myths on the question of how they represent the Oedipus complex (for references see Edmunds & Ingber, 1977).

It seems doubtful whether the Freudian version of the Oedipus complex really penetrates to the core of Sophocles' *Oedipus Tyrannus* and whether the Oedipus complex is the only possible direction of inquiry into these myths. Any science has not only to discern the way the essence of the studied phenomena manifests itself, but also to determine what the essence of these manifestations is. Accordingly we need not limit ourselves to Freud's concept of the Oedipus complex and can proceed to re-examine how the oedipal drama presents itself in the Oedipus myths. Freud notes that the latent content of these imaginative creations belongs to the "unconscious complexes of early childhood" (1925d, p. 69) consisting solely of "a reality experienced by the child" (1918b, p. 55). Thus, in Freud's conception the myths provide information about this reality in a mystified manner.

CHAPTER TWO

The abandonment of the seduction theory—reasons

> The foundation for a neurosis would accordingly always be laid in childhood by adults ....
>
> —Sigmund Freud, 1896c, pp. 208f

The seduction theory was published in 1896 in three essays (1896a; 1896b; 1896c). In these essays Freud put forward the idea that every hysteria goes along with "sexual experiences in childhood consisting in the stimulation of the genitals, coitus-like acts, and so on" (ibid., p. 206) that were "practised ... by adults who were strangers ... nursery maid or governess or tutor, or ... a close relative" and "brother and sister" (ibid., p. 207). A further indispensable "psychological precondition" for neurotic symptom formation is that these real infantile sexual scenes exist as *"unconscious memories"* (ibid., p. 211). The "hysterical symptoms are derivatives of memories which are operating unconsciously which ... only exercise a pathogenic action later, when they have been aroused ... in the form of unconscious memories" (ibid., p. 212; italics omitted).

In his famous letter to Fliess, dated 21 September 1897, Freud admits that his idea that every hysteria is based on real "sexual experiences in childhood" with other persons (1896c, pp. 206f.), was a fallacy. "I no longer believe in my *neurotica*", he writes and justifies this change by the "continual disappointments in my attempts at bringing an analysis to a real conclusion", the "absence of the complete successes", his "surprise at the fact that in every case the father, not excluding my own, had to be blamed as a pervert" and that "such a widespread extent of perversity towards children is, after all, not very probable," the "consideration that in the most deep-reaching psychosis the unconscious memory does not break through, so that the secret of childhood experiences is not disclosed even in the most confused delirium" and "the certain discovery that there are no indications of reality in the unconscious, so that one cannot distinguish between the truth and fiction that is cathected with affect" (1985c, pp. 259f.).

"Thus," he concludes, "the possibility remained open that sexual phantasy invariably seizes upon the theme of the parents" (ibid.). Looking back to these days in 1914 he states the same issue:

> If hysterical subjects trace back their symptoms to traumas that are fictitious, then the new fact which emerges is precisely that they create such scenes in phantasy, and this psychical reality requires to be taken into account alongside practical reality (Freud, 1914d, pp. 17f.).

It was the oedipal drama which was inherent in these phantasied scenes.

Many psychoanalysts are in agreement with Anna Freud who regards Freud's abandonment of the reality of seduction in favour of seduction fantasies as the birth of psychoanalysis. In a letter, dated 10 September 1981, Anna Freud writes to Masson:

> Keeping up the seduction theory would mean abandoning the Oedipus complex and with it the whole importance of conscious and unconscious fantasy. In fact, I think there would have been no psychoanalysis afterwards. (Masson, 1984, p. 113)

This view seems justified, because Freud's writings following the rejection of his seduction theory emphasise again and again that statements about sexual seductions are nothing but fantasies. For instance, writing on the subject of childhood seduction memories involving the father in 1916, he states that "there can be no doubt either of the imaginary nature of the accusation or of the motive that has led to it" (1916–1917a, p. 370). In 1933 he asserts unequivocally that the reports of "almost all my women patients ... that they had been seduced by their father ... were untrue", and "that hysterical symptoms are derived from phantasies and not from real occurrences" (1933a, p. 120). In this context Freud strongly rejects the ideas that Ferenczi presented in a lecture entitled "The passions of adults and their influence on the sexual and character development of children" (published under the title "Confusion of tongues between adults and the child") at the Congress in Wiesbaden in September 1932. In this lecture, Ferenczi (1932, p. 227) stated that "especially the sexual trauma, as the pathogenic factor cannot be valued highly enough", and that "children ... fall victim to real violence or rape much more often than one had dared to suppose." Ferenczi read this text to Freud on 30 August 1932 (Simon, 1992), and three days later Freud addressed a telegram to Eitington (cited in Sylwan, 1984, p. 109) stating "Ferenczi read me his paper. Harmless. Stupid .... Disagreeable impression," and on 3 September 1932 he wrote to his daughter that Ferenczi "had completely regressed to etiological views which I have been abed in, and gave up, 35 years ago" (cited in Gay, 1988, pp. 583–584).

Without entering into the controversy between Freud and Ferenczi in detail, we want to mention that, according to Simon (1992) in particular, Haynal (1988) believes that Freud's critical assessment—critical statements with regard to Ferenczi's lecture can also be found in Freud's telegram to Eitington, dated 2 September 1932 (cited in Sylwan, 1984, p. 109)—was mainly due to Ferenczi's technical treatment procedure. Haynal (1988, pp. 30f.) argues that Ferenczi's technical measures would have revived memories of Freud's experiences between Breuer and Anna O., and similarly difficult situations between Jung and Sabina Spielrein and between Elma Palos and Ferenczi. It is true that, as Izette de Forest, a patient of Ferenczi, told Erich Fromm (1959, pp. 63–65), when Ferenczi visited Freud before the Congress in Wiesbaden Freud disapproved of Ferenczi's "latest technical ideas" which he had presented to him, and that Freud criticised Ferenczi's (1932, p. 225) "regression in technique" in his letter to him, dated 2 October 1932, in which Freud refers to Ferenczi's lecture delivered at the congress. But Freud also questions the correctness of Ferenczi's findings. In trying to justify his request that Ferenczi should publish his lecture with a delay of one year, Freud states:

> I didn't want to give up hope that in your continuing work you would still recognize yourself the technical impropriety of your procedure and the limited correctness of your results. (Freud, 1992g, Vol. 3, p. 445)

Also there is no doubt that Freud's letter to his daughter confirms that his opposition definitely had to do with the importance Ferenczi ascribed to sexual childhood traumas (on this subject see also Masson, 1984; Rachman, 1997; Simon, 1992).

However, the reasons Freud used in his letter to Fliess to justify his predilection for fantasies rather than seduction are not as convincing as they may seem at first sight. His first argument, that of being unable to treat patients successfully, is not consistent with two of his other statements. First, when reasoning that in "some eighteen cases of hysteria I have been able to discover this connection [that sexual problems cause hysteria] and, where the circumstances allowed, to confirm it by *therapeutic success*", he stresses that he refers to "all the cases on which I have been able to carry out the work of analysis" (Freud, 1896c, pp. 199f.; our italics).[1] Second, two years later he writes: "I have in recent years almost completely worked out a therapeutic procedure which I propose to describe as 'psycho-analytic'. I owe a great number of *successes* to it" (1898a, p. 282; our italics). These two statements confirm Freud's satisfaction with his treatment success, thus conflicting with his own argument.

Freud's next argument, the implied high frequency of perversion against children, the premise that "all the fathers of hysteric patients must have been perverted" would certainly have been hard to verify. Yet Freud had already widened the field in that he also referred to other persons as possible seducers. Furthermore, Kupfersmid (1993) refers to Freud's statement that:

> I learnt from colleagues that there are several publications by paediatricians which stigmatise the frequency of sexual practices by nurses and nursery maids, carried out even on infants in arms; and in the last few weeks I have come across a discussion of "Coitus in Childhood" by Dr. Stekel (1895). (Freud, 1896c, p. 207)

Furthermore, Masson (1984) found in Freud's library books by Paul Bernard, Brouardel, and Tardieux in which the abuse of small children by adults was discussed. Kupfersmid (1993) and Masson (1984) emphasise that Freud was probably well aware of the high frequency of child abuse reported in the German and French literature of that time.

Freud's third argument, that psychotics would readily disclose their seduction if seduction theory was correct, cannot not stem from his own experiences as he only had a limited amount of clinical contact with psychotic individuals. Admittedly, in a letter to Fliess, dated 11 January 1897 (1985c, p. 222), Freud assumes that psychotics had been sexually abused before they were eighteen months old. Yet this assumption is based on one female psychotic individual who was not his own patient and did not talk about her seduction. Moreover, during this time period he only wrote about one case of psychosis (Freud, 1896b) in which the patient's report on his seduction could only be acquired with considerable effort on Freud's part.

Moreover, his argument is equally inconsistent with his assumption that in the case of a psychosis, that is,

> hysterical psychosis ... Amentia, or a confusional psychosis—a psychosis of being overwhelmed, ... sexual abuse occurs ... before the psychic apparatus has been completed in its first form (before the age of 1¼ to 1½ years). (Freud, 1985c, p. 222)

Just two weeks later he even suspects that in "hysterical psychosis" the sexual abuse occurs before the eleventh month of life (ibid., p. 226). Freud informed Fliess about these assumptions in his letters dated 9 and 24 January 1897, that is, about nine months before his letter of confession. Since it can hardly be justified to assume that patients are able to memorise and talk about traumas that had occurred before their "psychic apparatus has been completed," it is because of these assumptions that his argument loses its objective prerequisite.

In view of these contradictions, we query whether Freud really believed that the behaviour of psychotics had any significant relationship to the truth or falsehood of the seduction theory. Our doubts are shared by Kupfersmid (1993), who among others, refers to a letter to Fliess, dated 9 December 1899 (Freud, 1985c, p. 390). Freud writes that he had "long ago" given up differentiating neurosis from psychosis on the basis of the age at which seduction occurred and that psychosis was caused by masturbation.

Freud's methodical argument, that there are no indications of reality in the unconscious, similarly does not justify his turning to fantasies as an explanation. When a seduction becomes unconscious and is subsequently remembered and if there are no indications of reality in the unconscious, it cannot be determined whether a seduction has actually taken place in reality or was fantasised.

Similar to the arguments he puts forward in his letter to Fliess, the differing reasons that Freud gave in his publications are, as Kupfersmid in particular emphasises, equally unable to justify his rejection of his previous seduction theory. In 1905 Freud (1905d, pp. 190f.) argues that he learned that normal adults were sometimes sexually abused as children, although he had extensively discussed the lack of significance of this issue previously. Freud countered the observation "that there are numerous people who have a very clear recollection of infantile sexual experiences and who nevertheless do not suffer from hysteria" (1896c, p. 211) with the argument that in case of hysteria—as we already mentioned—the "scenes must be present as *unconscious memories*" (ibid.).

A year later he justifies his rejection of seduction with the argument that he had encountered an unusual sample of hysterical patients by chance (1906a, p. 274). Assuming for example, that at least two thirds of hysterics were not sexually abused and one third were, Kupfersmid (1993) points that the probability of having eighteen such patients in succession, just by chance, is over one million to one. It seems highly unlikely that Freud was convinced that he just happened to have such a highly atypical sample of hysterics.

In 1914 Freud thought that he might have been influenced by Charcot's view of the traumatic origin of hysteria (1914d, p. 17), but it is hard to imagine that Freud was convinced of being mislead by Charcot's traumatic theory of hysteria. He was well familiar with Charcot's idea that heredity causes hysteria and all other factors are merely potential precipitants of an underlying cerebral degeneracy, and in 1896 he had differentiated his view from that of Charcot quite clearly (Freud, 1896a, pp. 144ff.; 1896c, pp. 191ff.). After Charcot's death, Freud (1893f) summarised Charcot's position documenting his concerns about it:

> Charcot put forward a simple formula for this [traumatic hysteria]: heredity was to be regarded as the sole cause. Accordingly, hysteria was a form of degeneracy, a member of the *"famille névropathique"*.

All other aetiological factors played the part of incidental causes, of *"agents provocateurs"*. (Freud, 1893f, p. 21)

Freud added, "so greatly did Charcot overestimate heredity as a causative agent that he left no room for the acquisition of nervous illness" (ibid., p. 23).

Finally, in 1925 Freud suspected that patients' memories might be attributed to his therapeutic technique (1925d, p. 34). At first sight it seems as if this argument could be treated seriously. In a way similar to the way he constructed the latent content out of the manifest dream, he created the factual seduction out of the patients' stories and associations. Schimek (1975) points out that Freud was actively searching for the desired memories and in so doing, interpreted his data selectively. He held on to his interpretation even if his patients "unlike what happens in the case of other forgotten material [had] no feeling of remembering the scenes" (1896c, p. 204), so that one might conclude that Freud's self-critical objection might be genuine. However, it is unlikely that Freud really believed that his method was responsible for the patients' memories. In the very next paragraph, after suspecting a flaw in his clinical method, he writes: "I do not believe even now that I forced the seduction-phantasies on my patients, that I 'suggested' them" (1925d, p. 34).

Freud's conviction that he did not induce anything of what the patients memorised is also shown by his strict rejection of Fliess' criticism that "he read his own thoughts into the minds of his patients" (Meehl, 1994, p. 4). Freud answered in a letter to Fliess, dated 19 September 1901:

> If … you are ready to agree that the "reader of thoughts" perceives nothing in the other, but merely projects his own thoughts, you really are no longer my audience either and must regard my entire method of working as being just as worthless as the others do. (Freud, 1985c, p. 450)

Considering the doubtful nature of his reasoning, one can certainly conclude that Freud himself had doubts as to whether his arguments would justify abandoning the seduction theory. A letter to Fliess from 12 December 1897 three months after his confession supports this, stating "My confidence in paternal aetiology has risen greatly" (1985c, p. 286), [with "paternal aetiology" Freud refers to a seduction of girls by their fathers between the ages of eight and twelve years as the cause of neurosis (see letter to Fliess, 28 April 1897 ibid., p. 238)]. Further indications of seduction can also be found in his letters to Fliess from 5 November 1897 (ibid., p. 277), 22 December 1897 (ibid., p. 288), 10 March 1898 (ibid., p. 302), 27 April 1898 (ibid., p. 311), 27 September 1898 (ibid., p. 327), and in Freud (1898a, p. 280). Even eight years after his letter of confession to Fliess, Freud (1905d, p. 168) declares that "the sexual abuse of children is found with uncanny frequency among school teachers and child attendants" and that within the aetiology of neuroses in "the foreground we find the effects of seduction, which treats a child as a sexual object prematurely and teaches him, in highly emotional circumstances, how to obtain satisfaction from his genital zones" (1905d, p. 190). In 1916 he asserts that there are cases, "in which the whole weight of causation falls on the sexual experiences of childhood" (1916–1917a, p. 364), and that "Phantasies of being seduced are ... often ... not phantasies but real memories." In a 1924 addendum to "Further remarks on the neuro-psychoses of defence" in which he had also supported the seduction theory, he remarks that "we need not reject everything written in the text above. Seduction retains a certain aetiological importance, and even to-day I think some of these psychological comments are to the point" (1896b, p. 168). Seven years later he underlines once more that "Actual seduction ... is common enough" (1931b, p. 232; see also 1940a, p. 63).

Taking Freud's statements corporately, it seems likely that he did not completely abandon the seduction theory in 1897. Eissler (1993), Frampton (1991), Garcia (1987), Makari (1994), Sadow and colleagues (1976) and Simon (1992) argue that it was the claim to the universal validity of seduction that Freud discarded, the idea that every neurotic symptom necessarily presupposes a seduction in childhood. It is precisely the sense in which Freud argues in the above mentioned addendum where he states "I attributed to the aetiological factor of seduction a significance and universality which it does not possess" (Freud, 1896b, p. 168).

CHAPTER THREE

The invention of the Oedipus complex

> I venture to say that if psycho-analysis could boast of no other
> achievement than the discovery of the repressed Oedipus com-
> plex, that alone would give it a claim to be included among the
> precious new acquisitions of mankind.
>
> —Sigmund Freud, 1940a, pp. 191f

The significance and universality of manifest seduction in the aetiology of the neuroses became replaced by the significance and universality of the Oedipus complex.

In Draft N, dated 31 May 1897, Freud (1985c, p. 250) alluded to the oedipal situation stating that it "seems as though this death-wish is directed in sons against their father and in daughters against their mother". Reference to the oedipal setting appears, presumably for the first time, in a letter to Fliess, dated 15 October 1897, in which Freud discusses the progress of his self-analysis:[1]

> I have found, in my own case too, falling in love with the mother
> and jealousy of the father, and I now regard it as a universal event
> of early childhood ... If that is so, we can understand the riveting
> power of Oedipus Rex, in spite of all the objections ... the Greek

legend seizes on a compulsion which everyone recognizes because he feels its existence within himself. Each member of the audience was once, in germ and in phantasy, just such an Oedipus. (Freud, 1985c, p. 265)

With the provision that this complex is also valid for girls,[2] it appears in nearly the same wording in *The Interpretation of Dreams* (1900a, pp. 261–268). In a letter to Ferenczi, dated 28 June 1908 (1992g, p. 13), the oedipal theme is first addressed under the heading "Oedipus complex". Two years later it appears under this heading in published form (1910h, p. 171). In the same year, Freud underlines the oedipal conflict as the *"nuclear complex* of every neurosis" (1910a, p. 47) and in 1912, he localises this complex in the phylogenetic inheritance of mankind (1912–1913a, p. 160, p. 142). Because "Ontogenesis may be regarded as a recapitulation of phylogenesis" (Freud, 1915h, p. 131), the oedipal situation of an individual would repeat these dynamics. The universality of the Oedipus complex is justified by this heritage and is made explicit in a well-known footnote added to the *Three Essays on the Theory of Sexuality* in the 1920 edition: "Every new arrival on this planet is faced by the task of mastering the Oedipus complex; anyone who fails to do so falls a victim to neurosis" (1905d, p. 226). After stating that the "recognition ... of the Oedipus complex has become the shibboleth that distinguishes the adherents of psycho-analysis from its opponents" (ibid.), Freud underscores in the quotation at the beginning of this chapter the importance of the Oedipus complex for psychoanalysis at the end of his life.

It seems as if, even after the discovery of the Oedipus complex, Freud attributed to parental behaviour a function in sexual development, albeit not in form of manifest seductions. For example:

A child's intercourse with anyone responsible for his care affords him an unending source of sexual excitation and satisfaction from his erotogenic zones. This is especially so since the person in charge of him, who, after all, is as a rule his mother, herself regards him with feelings that are derived from her own sexual life: she strokes him, kisses him, rocks him and quite clearly treats him as a substitute for a complete sexual object. (1905d, p. 223)

And: "By her care of the child's body she [the mother] becomes his first seducer" (1940a, p. 65), who "by her activities over the child's bodily hygiene inevitably stimulated, and perhaps even roused for the first time, pleasurable sensations in her genitals" (1933a, p. 120). Even when presenting the oedipal setting, Freud emphasises the role played by the parents throughout the following references:

> The "affection" shown by the child's parents and those who look after him, which seldom fails to betray its erotic nature ("the child is an erotic plaything"), does a very great deal to raise the contributions made by erotism to the cathexes of his ego-instincts. (1912d, p. 181)

> [A] natural predilection usually sees to it that a man tends to spoil his little daughters, while his wife takes her sons' part ... The child is very well aware of this partiality and turns against that one of his parents who is opposed to showing it. (1900a, p. 258)

> The child takes both of its parents, and more particularly one of them, as the object of its erotic wishes. In so doing, it usually follows some indication from its parents, whose affection bears the clearest characteristics of a sexual activity, even though of one that is inhibited in its aims. As a rule a father prefers his daughter and a mother her son; the child reacts to this by wishing, if he is a son, to take his father's place, and, if she is a daughter, her mother's. (1910a, p. 47)

> The neurotic wife who is unsatisfied by her husband is, as a mother, over-tender and over-anxious towards her child, on to whom she transfers her need for love; and she awakens it to sexual precocity. The bad relations between its parents, moreover, excite its emotional life and cause it to feel love and hatred to an intense degree while it is still at a very tender age (1908d, p. 202)

> We must not omit to add that the parents themselves often exercise a determining influence on the awakening of a child's Oedipus attitude by themselves obeying the pull of sexual attraction, and that where there are several children the father will give the plainest evidence of his greater affection for his little daughter and the mother for her son. (1916–1917a, p. 333)

and:

> Incidentally, children often react in their Oedipus attitude to a stimulus coming from their parents, who are frequently led in their

preferences by difference of sex, so that the father will choose his
daughter and the mother her son as a favourite, or, in case of a
cooling-off in the marriage, as a substitute for a love-object that has
lost its value. (1916–1917a, p. 207)

At first sight these statements seem to indicate that Freud ascribes an
important role to the seductive tendencies of the parents in the development of the Oedipus complex. Since Freud assumes that the Oedipus
complex is universal, it seems obvious that the Oedipus complex of the
children is caused by an unconscious staging of the parents.

However, this is not Freud's view. He states succinctly that "the spon-
taneous nature of the Oedipus complex in children cannot be seriously
shaken" by the described parental behaviour (Freud, 1916–1917a, p. 333).
The influence of the parental unconscious is excluded, as Laplanche
(1986, p. 217) remarks, the origin of the Oedipus complex is localised in
the phylogenesis, and the parent's behaviour is reduced to "some sort
of impetus in the life of the individual" which the inherited "psychical
dispositions" have need of "before they can be roused into actual operation" (1912–1913a, p. 158).

CHAPTER FOUR

The myth of the primal horde

> I regard it as a methodological error to seize on a phylogenetic explanation before the ontogenetic possibilities have been exhausted. I cannot see any reason for obstinately disputing the importance of infantile prehistory while at the same time freely acknowledging the importance of ancestral prehistory.
>
> —Sigmund Freud, 1918b, p. 97

Freud mentions two reasons that forced him to base the Oedipus complex on phylogenetic factors. Firstly, to become effective, the fear of being castrated needs a "phylogenetic reinforcement" (Freud, 1926d, p. 147). This reinforcement can be put down to the fact "that during the human family's primeval period castration used actually to be carried out by a jealous and cruel father upon growing boys" (1933a, p. 86). Second, the

> behaviour of neurotic children towards their parents in the Oedipus and castration complex abounds in such reactions, which seem unjustified in the individual case and only become intelligible phylogenetically—by their connection with the experience of earlier generations. (1939a, p. 99)

19

Yet whether in Freud's understanding the efficacy of castration really needs such a reinforcement is not clear. Without mentioning or indicating such a reinforcement he regards it as sufficient for the effectiveness of castration-threat if the boy is convinced of the reality of castration by seeing the penis-less female genital (e.g., 1908c, p. 217; 1909b, p. 35; 1916–1917a, p. 370; 1918b, p. 45; 1925j, p. 252; 1927e, p. 154; 1931b, p. 229; 1940a, p. 190; 1940e, p. 276). It even seems as if Freud was not really convinced of the need for such a reinforcement. He states explicitly that the "scenes … of being threatened with castration … may just as easily be acquired by personal experience", and adds, as previously cited, that he regards "it as a methodological error to seize on phylogenetic explanation before the ontogenetic possibilities have been exhausted", and he stresses that he "cannot see any reason for obstinately disputing the importance of infantile prehistory while at the same time freely acknowledging the importance of ancestral prehistory" (1918b, p. 97).

In the light of the above mentioned methodological assertion Freud formulated seven years previously, namely that

> as long as it is possible for us to explain … things by an analysis of psychic phenomena, we are not justified in coming to the conclusion that a store of memories has been carried along phylogenetically. (Freud, 8 November 1911, Nunberg & Federn, 1974, p. 307)

It is equally doubtful whether the unjustified reactions of children in the oedipal situation necessarily support recourse to phylogenetic factors. Justification for such a recourse would require rejection of the ontogenetic influences on these reactions. If Freud had adhered to his own methodological advice, he would have been obliged to do what he refrained from doing, that is to say, to reject the theory of any influence of the parental unconscious on the apparently unjustified behaviour of the children.

One could go along with Fuchsman (2001, p. 114) in suspecting that the assumed universality of the Oedipus complex caused Freud to justify this complex phylogenetically. However, even in Freud's day existing knowledge contradicted this universality thesis and Freud was known to be familiar with the respective authors and their work (see e.g., Freud, 1931b, p. 242; 1963a, p. 105; Jones, 1957, p. 139; p. 254). Malinowski (1927) for instance, had found no trace of the classic Oedipus complex during his investigations of the Trobriands and this at least shed some doubts on Freud's thesis. Clark (1923) had reported on patients who had narcissistic disturbances without having an Oedipus complex and Fenichel (1931, p. 141) had referred to "cases of extreme malformation of character ... in which a true Oedipus complex has never become crystallized" (see also Bradley, 1926; Myers, 1926, cited in Brown, 1927). In the post-Freudian era, Loewald (1978) mentions patients with a borderline structure which cannot be understood on the basis of oedipal problems. Stoller (1985, p. 33) does not find an oedipal conflict in transsexual individuals and authors like Basch (1987), Beres and Obers (1950), Blos (1989), Gitelson (1952), Greenberg (1987), and Whitebook (1995) also disagree with Freud's thesis.[1]

In addition, the assumptions on which Freud's phylogenetic justification of the Oedipus complex is based are disputable. The ontogenetic emergence of the Oedipus complex is based on two assumptions, firstly that "Ontogenesis may be regarded as a recapitulation of phylogenesis" (Freud, 1915h, p. 131) and secondly that the Oedipus complex originates phylogenetically in the following event that would have been typed into the "archaic heritage" of mankind (1939a, p. 99): The primal father of the primal horde monopolised the females of the horde, forced his sons into sexual abstinence and expelled them. After a while, the frustrated sons united and killed the primal father. Since they felt guilty afterwards, they gave up putting their former incestuous wishes into action.

As early as in 1932 Reich (1932) argued that, as in the said primitive groupings sexual intercourse began a long time before puberty and on the assumption that sexually mature sons were banished, it was a mystery how these exiled children could have survived without care. Considering the relatively sparse population on earth in those prehistoric times, it would have been almost impossible for them to contact women from other groups. Why the group did not die out when the sons renounced sexual intercourse with their mother and sisters after killing the primal father was beyond comprehension. Furthermore, the Freudian thesis excluded the possibility of factual incest which was the rule rather than an exception in primeval times. Freeman (1967) and Wallace (1983) argue that no clues could be found indicating the ubiquitous existence of Freud's primal horde.

Moreover, Freud (1939a, p. 99) claims "that the archaic heritage of human beings comprises not only dispositions but also subject-matter—memory-traces of the experience of earlier generations", so that in his view, the course of ontogenesis is factually determined by archaic inheritance. However, the assumption that DNA-structure could be altered by virtue of mankind's psychic experiences and be passed down in the succession of generations was a controversial issue even in Freud's time (e.g., Mitchell, 1982) and has since been abandoned (e.g., Freeman, 1967; Moore & Fine, 1990, p. 147).

Furthermore, to reduce parental behaviour down to some vague kind of impetus instigates a further problem: if the Oedipus complex has a phylogenetic basis, excluding the parental unconscious from their interaction with the child would imply that the parents were capable of coping with their own Oedipus complex in a such way that it vanished out of their psychic life. Although Freud does not mention such a possibility in this context, in principle he seems in favour of such a possibility, which we will discuss in the next section.

CHAPTER FIVE

The myth of the dissolution of the Oedipus complex

> As far as normality is concerned, we have to acknowledge the persistence of life-time oedipal conflicts.
>
> —Serge Lebovici, 1982, p. 211

Freud mentions three circumstances under which the Oedipus complex can be destroyed.

- The Oedipus complex can perish because it is a "phenomenon which is determined and laid down by heredity and which is bound to pass away according to programme when the next pre-ordained phase of development sets in" (Freud, 1924d, p. 174). The "complex must collapse because the time has come for its disintegration, just as the milk-teeth fall out when the permanent one begin to grow" (ibid., p. 173).
- The Oedipus complex can pass away on account of "the experience of painful disappointments", the "absence of satisfaction", that is, due to its "lack of success" (ibid., p. 173).
- In boys the oedipal complex can be "smashed to pieces by the shock of threatened castration" (1924d, p. 175; 1925j, p. 25).

23

Freud's first argument is not consistent with his idea that the oedipal constellation is not dissolved in phylogenesis but is repressed and reappears, for instance, in the development of religion (e.g., Freud, 1939a, pp. 132f.). Since the developmental programme inscribed in the "archaic heritage" (ibid., p. 99) does not foresee the dissolution of the Oedipus complex, the milk-teeth hypothesis is not tenable.

His second argument stands in contradiction to his phylogenetic postulate that the origin of the Oedipus complex is due to the primal father causing the sons' frustration. If ontogenesis recapitulates phylogenesis, it is hardly possible that in ontogenesis the Oedipus complex is resolved by the same kind of experiences that have caused this complex in phylogenesis. Also, this argument is not compatible with Freud's concept of fixation. Fixations are the outcome of "frustration" (1912c, p. 231) and frustrations cannot be the reason for both adhering to and for giving up instinctual desires. In addition, his thesis that the Oedipus complex can perish is incompatible with his general postulate "that in mental life nothing which has once been formed can perish—that everything is somehow preserved" (1930a, p. 69; see also 1937d, p. 259).

His third argument is at odds with other considerations. Freud argues that in the process, in which the Oedipus complex is "smashed to pieces by the shock of threatened castration" (Freud, 1925j, p. 257), the "authority of the father or the parents is introjected and forms the nucleus of the super-ego ... and so secures the ego from the return of the libidinal object-cathexis" (1924d, pp. 176f.). This view is in agreement with the idea that "the sexual ties of the earliest years of childhood ... persist, though repressed and unconscious" (1921c, p. 138). However, it is not consistent with the idea that the "object-cathexes are given up" (1924d, p. 176). If the oedipal object-cathexes disappeared, there would be no need for a super-ego that "secures the ego from the return of the libidinal object-cathexis" (ibid., p. 177).

Furthermore, the superego is understood as the "heir of the Oedipus complex" (1925d, p. 39). If the oedipal wishes do not exist any more, the fear of castration must disappear too. Since the "nucleus round which the subsequent fear of conscience has gathered" is to be seen in the "dread of castration" (1923b, p. 57), where does the power with which the superego succeeds in asserting its demands then come from?

In Freud's conception the destruction of the Oedipus complex cannot be determined conclusively. This might have been one of the reasons why Jones (1957, p. 259) and other psychoanalysts were greatly surprised at Freud's assertion "that the Oedipus wishes are not merely repressed, but are actually destroyed and annulled." Jones critically remarks that in this case "unconscious impulses could undergo such a fate, one surely never encountered in analytic praxis" (ibid.). Bergmann (1988), Burgner (1985), Etchegoyen (1993), Furman (1988), Lebovici (1982), and Loewald (1979) also argue that oedipal wishes cannot perish by themselves.

But even if the Oedipus complex cannot be annulled, the consequence is not necessarily the development of a symptom neurosis, as Freud (1905d, p. 226) claims. Within his conceptual framework, symptom neurosis can be prevented by creating sublimations of the Oedipus complex (1924d, p. 177). Without entering into a critical debate of that concept, we just want to point out that along with Freud, who, as Waelder (1963, pp. 122f.) reports, "took the view that 'sublimation' was not a well-defined psychic mechanism like repression or reaction formation but rather a loose characterisation of various processes that lead to socially more valuable activities" we understand sublimation as "only a special case of the way in which sexual trends are attached to other, non-sexual ones" (Freud, 1916–1917a, p. 345), as a "displacement of instinctual aims ... to a so-called 'higher' level" (Anna Freud, in J. Sandler & Anna Freud, 1983, p. 83; see also Hartmann, 1955, p. 10; Vaillant, 1992, p. 39). Both definitions indicate that sublimation should not be seen as a specific mechanism of defence but as specific substitutive formation.

If we take a look at the example of religion Freud uses to explain such a displacement of former instinctual aims into culturally acceptable and conscious substitutive formations, it is immediately evident that such an operation must forbid any exclusion of the parental unconscious in conceptualising the infant's socialisation. On the contrary, the answer to the question "How is the Oedipus complex established in the child?" is a direct invitation to include the oedipal problems of the parents. In the case of religion, the individual condenses the existing "store of religious ideas" (Freud, 1927c, p. 42) with "conflicts of its childhood arising from the father-complex ... which it has never wholly overcome" (1927c, p. 30), and transfers them in the guise of culturally approved substitutive formations into a form "which is universally accepted" (1927c, p. 30). By virtue of this condensation of warded-off conflicts into prevailing cultural forms of interaction, the individuals spare "the task of constructing a personal ... neurosis" (1927c, p. 44). They do not become "asocial" as Freud (ibid.) terms symptom neuroses, but remain social in that they join with others in "usual group formations" [in German: *habituelle Massenbildungen*] (1921c, p. 142). That is to say, in the guise of conscious, socially approved substitutive formations, the parents' unconscious oedipal problems can enter into culturally licensed forms such as child care and education.

CHAPTER SIX

Oedipus myths

> If Freud's interpretation is right, we should expect the myth to
> tell us that Oedipus met Jocasta without knowing that she was
> his mother, fell in love with her, and than killed his father, again
> unknowingly. But there is no indication whatsoever in the myth
> that Oedipus is attracted by or falls in love with Jocasta.
> —Erich Fromm, 1957, p. 121

The different configurations of the oedipal drama in Greek mythology
of which Freud was probably familiar with also remain unconsidered.
Most of them are mentioned in Roscher's *Lexikon der griechischen und
römischen Mythologie* and in Preller's *Griechische Mythologie*, and Freud
quotes both sources in his writings (e.g., Freud, 1901b, p. 218; 1910c,
p. 88; 1913f, p. 298). Devereux (1953) refers to many Greek sources
with the following narrative: Laius, who had no desire for children on
account of the oracle's verdict, is first made drunk and then seduced
by Jocasta; the fight between Laius and Oedipus occurs in the presence of Jocasta who encourages Oedipus and the incest[1] occurs shortly
after the murder of Laius. In another version Laius is portrayed as the
originator of pederasty who falls violently in love with Chrysippus
before his marriage to Jocasta, kidnapping, raping him, and fostering a

27

homosexual relationship with him. In yet another version, the oracle of Delphi's prediction that Laius' own son will kill him and replace him in Jocasta's bed is attributed to Pelops, who wanted retaliation for Laius' violations of his son (Licht, 1912, p. 134; Roscher, 1884–1890, p. 903; 1897–1909, p. 703).

The differing versions of the Oedipus myth allow us to detect the homosexual background of the Oedipus complex (Kouretas, 1975, p. 366) in Greek mythology. Devereux (1953) and Ross (1982) argue that the piercing of Oedipus' ankles with a nail and the swordfight that Laius starts with Oedipus can be understood as symbolic representations of homosexual interactions. Devereux (1953) takes this up in pointing out that after killing Laius, Oedipus deprives him of both his sword and his belt (see Gruppe, 1906a, p. 522; Robert, 1915, p. 160; Roscher, 1897–1909, p. 714; Schneiderhan, 1852, p. 30). In ancient Greece, the undoing of a woman's belt was a preliminary to intercourse, and Devereux (1953, p. 134) concludes that when sleeping with Oedipus, Jocasta "represented both herself and the castrated and feminised Laius".

In the following, we will take the roles of Laius and Jocasta in the myths into more detailed consideration and discuss the consequences which follow from them.

Laius

The oracle of Delphi plays a central role in Sophocles' drama *Oedipus Tyrannus*. The oracle predicts that Laius' son will kill him and replace him in his wife's bed. This prophecy is the starting point of the drama. When the prophecy is attributed to Pelops, the structure of the drama changes qualitatively. Although this attribution has been noticed by several authors (e.g., Constans, 1881, p. 26; Devereux, 1953; Kerènyi, 1959, p. 89; Licht, 1912, p. 134; Lidz, 1988; Pollock, 1986; Preller, 1875, p. 347; Priel, 2002; Roscher, 1884–1890, p. 903; 1897–1909, p. 703; Rosenman, 1982), neither Freud nor the post Freudian era reacted to the resulting change in the structure of the drama. The structural change comes about by virtue of Pelops, the father of Chrysippus, entering into the drama (Licht, 1912, p. 134; Preller, 1875, p. 343; Roscher, 1897–1909, p. 703) and Chrysippus himself being understood as Oedipus' alter ego (Devereux, 1953; Rosenman, 1982; Ross, 1982). Chrysippus is Pelops' dearly beloved son, who was conceived either with the nymph Axioche or with Danais (Roscher, 1884–1890, p. 741, p. 902). Alike Chrysippus, who is Pelops' illegitimate son, Oedipus is an adopted son of Polybus. In one version of the myth, Polybus' wife presents Oedipus to Polybus as her own child (Gruppe, 1906a, p. 509; Schneiderhan, 1852, p. 36). In other versions, Chrysippus is killed by Pelops (Roscher, 1884–1890, p. 904) as Laius attempts to kill Oedipus, Oedipus then kills Laius when he tries to help Chrysippus after his being kidnapped by Laius (Gruppe, 1906a, p. 509; Roscher, 1897–1909, p. 711).

The Oedipus drama acquires a different character if the source of the prophecy is an oracle. In this case the fate of the mortals is predetermined by the gods and as such is inescapable. In Pelops' case the prophecy becomes "in actual fact the voice of the Father" (Simonsuuri, 1993, p. 3).

This personalisation of the oracle exists in the eldest version of the Oedipus drama. Robert (1915, p. 69) indicates that the drama existed long before the dominant position of the Delphic oracle was established and argues that in the oldest versions, Teiresias was believed to have foreseen the fate of Laius in a dream of Laius (or in a dream of another person).

As Ross (1982) points out, the personalisation of the prophecy expresses the father's fear of his son's revenge for what he has done to him. The subsequent introduction of the oracle of Delphi into the oedipal drama suggests that this introduction may have served to conceal the real state of affairs and to mystify the fears of the father as an inescapable fate. As the concealed issue always reappears in the subject in which it is concealed, it is hardly surprising that the father's murderous intention can be traced to the oracle of Delphi. In Sophocles (2010) *ΟΙΔΙΠΟΥΣ ΤΥΡΑΝΝΟΣ* [*Oedipus Tyrannus*], Oedipus asks the Herdsman about the prophecy on account of which he was to kill the baby that the mother had given to him. The Herdsman answers: "Κτενεῖν νιν τοὺς τεκόντας ἦν λόγος".[2] D. Van der Sterren (1974, p. 128; translated for this edition) points out that "τοὺς τεκόντας" relates to both parents and that the oracle can be read as "'he will kill his parents' as well as 'his parents will kill him'".

As the myth continues, it states that on account of Pelops' prophecy, the descendants of Labdacus, Laius, and Oedipus, will suffer all the misfortunes to come (Constans, 1881, p. 26; Preller, 1921, p. 884; Roscher, 1884–1890, p. 903). Demystified, Oedipus' misfortune is not caused by an anonymous and fatefully penetrating power, but by the fear of the father. Oedipus does not wish to eliminate his father, on the contrary, the father wishes to eliminate his son and so sets the drama in motion.[3]

As A. Rascovsky and M. Rascovsky (1972) note, filicide by fathers is well known and is not confined to the Oedipus myths. The Lederer (1967), Mann (1993), Money-Kyrle (1939), Rank (1926), and Squire (1975) refer to Babylonian and Sumerian, German, Native American, Celtic, Persian, and other Greek myths in which fathers kill their sons. We will name some of the myths these authors have mentioned. Tanatus, to test the gods' omnipotence, served them the flesh of his own son Pelops to see if they could distinguish it from the flesh of some beast. Zeus, perceiving the deception that had been practiced, ordered that the flesh be put back into the cauldron and the child restored to life (Mann, 1993). King Aun of Sweden sacrificed one of his sons every ninth year to Odin, for he could only live as long as he fulfilled the sacrifice Odin demanded (Lederer, 1967). In the Icelandic-Norwegian saga King Jörmunrek courts Svanhild upon the advice of his confidant Bikki. His son, Randver, fetches the bride, and Bikki tells the King that they are guilty of having a sexual relationship. Jörmunrek has his son hanged and Svanhild trampled to death by wild horses (Rank, 1926, p. 133).

In American Indian myth, the sun father chases and eats his star-children because he needs their light to feed his own radiance, which is why they cannot be seen during the day; once a month the moon-mother draws a dark veil across her face in mourning for her dead children (Mann, 1993). Furthermore, in a Celtic myth Cuchulainn kills his son Conloch unknowingly with an invisible spear, and his wife, Emer, suspecting this relationship, wants to stop him (Mann, 1993). Finally, Mann (1993) refers to the biblical story of Abraham and Isaac and the crucifixion of Jesus, God's sacrifice of his own son and concludes: "The father is seeing the boy as a rival from the beginning of his life, and this is what brings the father to the initial oedipal rivalry" (ibid., p. 58).[4]

The fact that in Greek myths, the father's brutality is the reason for the son's violence against him, is probably not so well-known. For instance, Uranus throws his sons into the Underworld, Cronus, persuaded by his mother Gaia, releases them, overthrows Uranus and castrates him on behalf of his mother. In turn, Cronus devours his offspring after birth as he is afraid that his own children will overthrow him. Cronus is later overthrown by his youngest son Zeus, who was hidden away from him by his mother Rhea (Graves, 1955, p. 37ff.).

Both of these myths not only show that the son's violence against his father is a reaction to his father's brutality. They also show that in forming an oedipal configuration the violent reactions of the sons, Cronus and Zeus, are supported by their mothers, Gaia and Rhea.

According to the myths, the father's rivalry with his son stems from the father's own history. The relationship between Uranus and Cronus repeats itself in the relationship between Cronus and Zeus. As a child, Laius is expelled from Thebes by Zethus and Amphion, the twin sons of Antiope, but later returns and wins back the throne after the death of the twins (Devereux, 1953; Ross, 1982). Just as Jocasta exposes Oedipus, Antiope exiles Amphion and Zethus on Mount Cithaeron (Lidz, 1988; Roscher, 1884–1890, p. 381f.). They later return and regain the throne of Thebes from Lycus who had usurped the king's throne after the death of Labdacus.

Relating these myths to the oedipal situation, one can conclude that the father competes with his son for the love of the mother because of his own oedipal problems. He intends to eliminate his son as a male rival and thus threatens him with castration. As a boy, his own father had competed with him and threatened him with castration. The boy identified with his father and now actively repeats the events that he had experienced passively with his father with his own son.

In light of this interpretation of the prophecy, Laius' piercing of Oedipus' ankles and Oedipus' exposure, indicating the intention of letting the child die, both symbolise the father's castrating tendency (e.g., Devereux, 1953; Fernando, 1998; Rank, 1926, p. 218).

Jocasta

As mentioned previously, Jocasta's knowledge that Oedipus is in fact her son is implicit in Sophocles' drama. Taking note that the myths mention Jocasta's passion for Oedipus (Preller, 1921, p. 894), yet neither in Sophocles' drama nor in the myths is there any indication whatsoever that Oedipus is attracted to Jocasta (Fromm, 1957, p. 121), this knowledge amounts to a revelation of the mother's secret seduction of her son. If one argues that Oedipus acts for unconscious reasons, the absence of manifest information about an attraction would be understandable. However, given the view that repression "as a rule … creates a substitutive formation" (Freud, 1915d, p. 154), there still would have to be evidence that could be interpreted as an indirect representation of his interest in Jocasta. But even such indirect evidence is missing.

The context in which Oedipus solves the riddle of the Sphinx cannot allow us to interpret his solution as having the intention of winning the widowed Queen (e.g., Edmunds, 1988). The Sphinx was a monster that terrorised the Thebans. She consisted of "a woman's head, lion's body, serpent's tail, and eagle's wings" (Graves, 1955, p. 372).[5] The only means of saving Thebes was to solve her riddle. The Sphinx devoured everyone who failed to find a solution for the riddle and if the riddle was solved, the Sphinx would die. Since nobody was able to solve the riddle, the Council of Thebes promised that the one who solved the riddle and freed the Thebans from the Sphinx would be rewarded by the widowed Queen and become King of Thebes. Oedipus solved the riddle, the Sphinx committed suicide, Jocasta took him to be her husband and he became King of Thebes.

There are other grounds which justify the existence of the Sphinx in the oedipal drama. One possible reason is that Hera sent the Sphinx to Thebes as a punishment for Laius' rape of and love affair with Chrysippus (Graves, 1955, p. 372; Gruppe, 1906a, p. 522; Mann, 1993; Pollock, 1986; Stewart, 1961). Robert (1915, p. 63) does not agree, arguing that it makes no sense not to let the Sphinx appear until after Laius' death and have his dependents continue to suffer from the Sphinx if the Sphinx is to be thought of as a punishment for Laius' misdemeanour.

Gruppe (1906a, pp. 523f.) proposes another reason, namely that the Sphinx and her riddle were added to the Oedipus myth at a later date. In Homer's epics there is no reference to the Sphinx, and he assumes that the Sphinx' introduction serves to make the incest appear more horrific. Perhaps the Sphinx could also serve to make the incest less obvious. As such attempts never totally succeed and the concealed issue somehow always manages to emerge in the attempts to conceal it, the reappearance of the veiled relationship between Jocasta and Oedipus in the relationship between the Sphinx[6] and Oedipus would seem to support this idea. Caldwell (1974), Kanzer (1950), Rank (1926, p. 216), M. Rascovsky (1968), Schmidt (1877, p. 143), Shengold (1963), Stewart (1961), and H. A. Van der Sterren (1952) understand the Sphinx to be a manifestation of aspects of Jocasta and in the myths, similar behaviours are attributed to the Sphinx and to Jocasta. Reik (1920, p. 24) refers to myths in which the Sphinx is intended to represent the queen. Rank (1926, p. 216) mentions other myths in which the queen herself poses the riddle to be solved by the candidates. Another myth tells us that after her crime is discovered, Jocasta commits suicide by jumping off a cliff in the same way as the sphinx does when her riddle is solved (Graves, 1955, p. 376). Gruppe (1906a, p. 523) mentions a myth in which Oedipus kills the male lover of the Sphinx and approaches the Sphinx sexually.

H. A. Van der Sterren (1952, p. 347) underlines another similarity between Jocasta and the Sphinx. In both cases Oedipus is faced with a riddle whose solution as well as its non-solution have death as a consequence. In Jocasta's case, the Thebans are going to die if the riddle of Laius' death is not solved and if it is solved, then Jocasta dies. In the case of the Sphinx, the Thebans die if they do not succeed in solving the riddle of the Sphinx, but if they find the solution, then the Sphinx dies.

If we consider the latent content of the riddle's solution that Edmunds (1988) and Stewart (1961) provide us with, we find further reference to the identity of Jocasta and the Sphinx. The riddle is:

> What being, with only one voice, has sometimes two feet, some-
> times three, sometimes four, and is weakest when he has the most?
> (Graves, 1955, p. 372)

Oedipus knows the answer:

> Man ... because he crawls on all fours as an infant, stands firmly
> on his two feet in his youth, and leans upon a staff in his old age.
> (ibid.)

The riddle and its solution have been interpreted in various ways. It has been understood as "an expression of man's curiosity turned upon himself" (Bion, 1963, p. 62), as presenting "problems of both sexuality and mortality" (Caldwell, 1974, p. 215), as an "allegory of the problems presented by female sexuality" (Kanzer, 1950, p. 562), "as a description of sexual intercourse" (1964, p. 35). In Freud's (1925d, p. 37) view it puts "the question of where babies come from" and according to Rado the riddle represents the

> sexual act of the parents (4 legs); from the embrace of the parents is
> born the child (2 legs); grown to maturity, the boy develops a third
> (sexual) member (3 legs). (Rado, 1956, p. 229)

In Róheim's understanding the riddle relates to the primal scene, as it is seen by the child:

> Two people lie in one bed. The observer first sees four legs (*i.e.*, the father on all fours); then the two outstretched legs of the mother and finally one leg which ... mysteriously disappears. (Róheim, 1934, p. 7)

The Sphinx itself is the solution of the riddle because the Sphinx represents "father and mother in one person" (ibid., p. 8), that is, "two people in the act of intercourse" (Money-Kyrle, 1939, p. 39).

However, these interpretations of the riddle's latent content fail to disclose why the Sphinx commits suicide when her riddle is solved.

Edmund (1988) and Stewart (1961) provide us with an interpretation which makes the Sphinx's suicide understandable. Edmunds (1988, p. 54), refers to Lévi-Strauss (1973, p. 34; Edmunds' translation), in which Lévi-Strauss proposes the following homology between incest and riddle:

> Like the solved riddle, incest brings together terms destined to remain separate: the son is united to the mother, the brother to the sister just as the answer [to the riddle] *does in succeeding, contrary to all expectations, in reuniting itself with its question.* (Lévi-Strauss, 1973, p. 34)

Edmunds understands the formal procedure of riddle-solving as a mystification of the incest. Therefore, "the marriage to Jocasta ... is ... prefigured" in the riddle-solving (Edmunds, 1988, p. 54).

In Stewart's (1961) conception Oedipus' solution represents the ways Jocasta has treated him in the past and intends to treat him in the future, first by abandoning him as an infant, then using him to kill her husband and finally as a mate:

> These three modes may represent a fresh answer to the riddle of the Sphinx—first as a newborn infant with four legs in the morning, then as a warrior with two legs in the afternoon, and then as a lover with three legs in the evening—not an old man with a stick but a young man with a penis. (Stewart, 1961, p. 429)

In Edmunds and Stewarts interpretations Oedipus reveals Jocasta's secrets both in the riddle and its solution. That is to say, the Sphinx commits suicide for the same reason as Jocasta,[7] in other words, the death of the Sphinx becomes understandable if Jocasta and the Sphinx are regarded as one person.

Collectively, these myths suggest that in all likelihood, Oedipus' ability to solve the Sphinx' riddle was not solely due to his cleverness. As we aforementioned, it was declared that the one who solved the riddle of the Sphinx would marry Queen Jocasta and rule Thebes (Roscher, 1897–1909, p. 715). One might suspect that Jocasta, who also appears as a priestess of the Sphinx (Graves, 1955, p. 375), knew the answer to the riddle and told it to Oedipus. It is true that in *Oedipus Tyrannus*, Oedipus contends that he has solved the riddle just by using his common sense (Sophocles, 1991a, 398). Yet it is also true that the priest states "it was God that aided you, men say" (ibid., 38) and that in the myth, Oedipus receives divine help (Roscher, 1897–1909, p. 718). In light of Thebes' proclamation, by telling Oedipus the correct answer Jocasta was able to fulfil her incestuous wishes without them being recognised as such. Thus, the introduction of the Sphinx into the oedipal drama really helped to hide Jocasta's incestuous intentions.

Other myths have the similar notion that it is not primarily the sons who approach their mother with incestuous intentions. Nero, for example, is seduced by his mother Agrippina, Semiramis wants to sleep with her son (Rank, 1926, p. 57), and in the tale of "Periander" (ibid., pp. 394f.) it is told that the mother of Periander develops a fierce passion for her son when he is very young, initially satisfying her desire by hugging the boy intensively. When her son gets older she decides as a consequence of her rising passion to tell him that a very beautiful married woman loves him and wants to meet him. At first, Periander refuses because meetings with married women are forbidden by law but his mother insists and he finally agrees. On the night that the mother arranged for the meeting, she tells him not to light any lamp in the chamber and not to let the woman speak. Periander promises to follow all his mother's instructions. At night she decorates herself in beautiful attire and visits her son but makes sure that she leaves before morning. The following day she asks him whether he was satisfied and whether he wants the woman to come to him again. Periander answers that he desires it very much and that he had had great pleasure. From this time on, his mother constantly visits her son in the same way. Because Periander develops loving feelings he wants to find out the identity of this person, but his mother won't answer his questions. So one night, when she is there, he lights up a lamp in the room. When he sees that it is his mother who has been visiting him, he is so enraged that he wants to kill her and it is only the entrance of a demonic apparition that prevents him from so doing. From that time on, Periander becomes confused and cruel in nature, victimising many of his fellow citizens. In distress over her own fate, the mother commits suicide (more examples in Freemantle, 1950; Rank, 1926, pp. 348f.).

Another example is the Arab legend in which the son of Kena'an and Salchâ gets exposed by his parents because of a frightening prophecy. They hoped he would die and thus bring his father no harm, but he was miraculously saved and suckled by a female tiger and later he was raised by the inhabitants of a nearby village. When he grew up, he gathered together a great army and fought against his unrecognised father, Kena'an, whom he killed in a decisive battle. In triumph he entered the capital city and married his mother Salchâ (ibid., pp. 348f.).

We find another account of incest between mother and son in a myth taken from *Gesta Romanorum* (Constans, 1881, p. 125). An emperor had a beautiful wife, whom he loved very much. In the first year of their marriage she bore him a son, whom she loved very much, and whom she even slept with each night. When the child was three years old, the emperor died. The queen mourned his death for many days. After her husband was buried, she lived in a palace and had her son with her. She loved the boy so much that she could not do without his presence. They always slept together until the boy was eighteen. When the Evil One noticed this intense love between mother and son he tempted her into sin and to have intercourse with her son. The queen conceived immediately, but while she was pregnant, her son, in desolation, left the kingdom and proceeded to distant lands. In the meantime, the mother gave birth to a very beautiful boy but immediately after his birth she murdered him by cutting his throat.

In another myth, which Constans (1981, pp. 121f.) mentions, a widow, tempted by the devil, repeatedly has intercourse with her son. The son goes to the pope to confess their sin; the Holy Father keeps him there. In the meantime, the mother gives birth to a daughter with whom she also goes to Rome to receive forgiveness from the pope. There she meets her son and the pope commands them each to wander through the world alone, wearing cowhides. They may only show hands, feet, and face. After seven years they meet again. All three die in one night, amid miraculous phenomena.

Here we can include the legend of Judas which we mentioned previously and which was probably recorded around about 1260 by Jacobus de Voragine (Freemantle, 1950). Reuben and his wife Cyborea lived in Jerusalem. One night Cyborea dreams that she is about to conceive, and that her child will be the downfall of his people. After the child's birth his parents, to avoid killing him directly, decide to expose him in a chest on the sea. Wind and waves bring him to the island of Scariot. There he is found by the childless queen of the island and raised as her own child. Thus Judas was brought up in royal fashion as heir to the kingdom. But before very long it comes about that the royal pair have a son of their own and the foundling has to take his place behind the legitimate child. Judas treats the preferred competitor with meanness and envy and finally murders him. For fear of the consequences he flees and takes a ship heading for Jerusalem, finds a position at the court of Pilate and becomes Pilate's "boon companion" (ibid., p. 408). Pilate makes him his closest confidant and places him in charge of his whole household. One day, having developed an insatiable craving, Pilate has him fetch some fine apples from a nearby orchard. Thereby an argument arises between Judas and the owner of the garden. Judas slays his opponent in great anger with a stone, not knowing that his opponent is his father, Reuben. Pilate rewards Judas with the orchard and the murdered man's widow, who believes that her husband has died a natural death. Cyborea is extremely unhappy and sighs frequently. When asked one day by her husband what the cause of her grief is, she reveals enough of her story to enable Judas to recognise his double crime of parricide and incest. Deeply remorseful, he takes his mother's advice, goes to the Saviour and confesses his deeds. Jesus receives him with love and makes him an apostle (Rank, 1926, p. 277f.).

In all these examples, either the mothers seduce their sons, or the son is brought to his mother by fate. There is no myth in which the son yearns for his mother with incestuous intentions.

These myths lead us to hunt for the reasons for mothers seducing their sons in their past history. In one mythological version, Jocasta is suspected of having had an incestuous relationship with her father, Menoeceus (Stewart, 1961) and it seems that even this incest had a precedent. In another myth, Menoeceus appears as a "Sown Man" because he rises from the earth when Cadmus sows the serpent's (Graves, 1955, p. 373) or dragon's teeth (Parsons, 1990), and Jocasta is portrayed as a mythical figure stemming from "mother earth" (Robert, 1915, p. 111, p. 44; translated for this edition) or as the "humanised earth goddess" (Preller, 1921, p. 879; translated for this edition). If the earth is the "all-mother" (in German: "Allmutter"), the sons of the earth are naturally at the same time husbands to the mother (Robert, 1915, p. 45). That is to say, Jocasta is the offspring of incest. In Greek mythology, incest is understood "as the human counterpart of the primal and ever-renewed fecundity of the earth" (Edmunds, 1988, p. 61); thus, the incest between Menoeceus and Jocasta, between father and daughter, repeats an incestuous act between mother and son, which then reappears as the incest of Jocasta and Oedipus.[8]

We find a combination of a father-daughter and mother-son incest in a Cypriot folktale. A man has three daughters which he cannot marry off. He lives on the seashore, in a place where ships moor, and affixes the pictures of his three daughters on the door of his house to attract suitors. A captain appears who wishes to marry the youngest of the three daughters, Rosa, and he receives her hand in marriage. But on the night of his wedding, when he is about to go to bed with his wife, a ghost appears telling him to keep away from his wife, for she is destined to bear a son to her father and later to marry the son. Thereafter the captain asks for the eldest daughter and receives her hand in marriage. The same thing happens to another man, who also relinquishes Rosa and marries her second sister. A short while later, Rosa asks the elder sister to let her take her place in bed with her husband for one night. The sister refuses and Rosa discovers the reason for this rejection. She goes to her second sister and asks the same favour, also without success. Finally she decides to eliminate her father in order to prevent the fulfilment of the prophecy and has him killed by peasants.

On the grave of the father, buried in a distant land, there grows an apple tree. Rosa eats the fruit of this tree without knowing its origin and becomes pregnant. When she hears that there is an apple tree standing on her father's grave, she understands how she became pregnant and decides to kill the child as soon as it is born. After his birth, she stabs her son several times in the chest and places him in a little box, which she throws into the sea. The boy is found and raised by a sea captain. During a journey which the boy is undertaking to carry on his foster father's business, he arrives in his mother's country. He hears the story of the three sisters and marries one, his mother, and sires children with her. The scars on his breast reveal his identity. Rosa, seeing that the prophecy has been fulfilled, throws herself from the roof of the house and is killed (Rank, 1926, pp. 297f.).

Like the violence of the fathers towards their sons and the sons' revenge, the father-daughter incest is not restricted to the Oedipus myths. In Rank's view (ibid., p. 300), in the majority of the stories incest is initiated on the part of the father. For example, Zeus sleeps with his daughter Persephone in the shape of a snake and fathers Bacchus or Dionysos (Roscher, 1897–1909, p. 1140), and Odin fathers Thor with his daughter Yord (Rank, 1926, p. 302). In the legend of Clymenus, Clymenus has two sons and a daughter, Harpalyce. She is very beautiful and Clymenus falls in love with her. Initially he attempts to master his passion, but later, with the help of her nursemaid, he sleeps with her. Soon after she has married Alstor, Clymenus pursues them and abducts his daughter in Argos, where he takes her by force in public view. In revenge, Harpalyce kills her younger brother and serves him to her father as a meal. Upon her request, she is transformed into a bird, and Clymenus kills himself on becoming aware of her terrible revenge (ibid., p. 304).

In the myth of King Antiochus, his wife dies when his beautiful daughter reaches marriageable age. While many princes suit for the beautiful and virtuous girl, the father himself falls passionately in love with her and one day he rapes her. Then he ponders how he can keep the princes at bay and enjoy his daughter undisturbed. He proclaims that whoever desires to marry his daughter must first prove his wisdom sufficiently enough to be his successor in his kingdom. A riddle has to be solved. Anyone who takes the challenge but can't find the solution to the riddle must be subject to his sword. Many princes fall victim to the cruelty of the father, because he discourages the applicants by also killing those who provided the correct answer (ibid., p. 305).

An Armenian tale drastically illustrates how the father attempts to protect his daughter from the advances of other men. Assly, daughter of a priest is trapped from head to toe in an enchanted, impenetrable, irremovable, indestructible gown. It is studded from top to bottom with a long row of buttons; each one fastens by itself as soon as the next one is undone. Assily's father wove and prepared this gown himself, and he alone was able to overcome the magic of his daughter's gown (ibid., pp. 314f.).

What impresses one most about these myths, is that the daughters are described as passive objects of destiny or of the father's seduction. The few legends in which the incest is staged by the daughter lead Rank (ibid. p. 300) to premise that this is just a justification for the father's attempts to shift the blame for the seduction onto the daughter. For example, in the tale of Myrrha, Myrrha is supposed to have been inflamed by Aphrodite with love for her father. With the help of her nursemaid she tricks her father into believing she is a different woman for twelve nights in succession. When he finally recognises his daughter, he pursues her with a drawn sword. Myyrha begs the Gods to spare her and is transformed into a tree. Ten months later, the tree bursts and Adonis came into the world (Roscher, 1884–1890, pp. 71f.). In another myth, Adonis is born out of a tree when Myrrha's father splits this tree with a sword (Rank, 1926, p. 302).

CHAPTER SEVEN

Freud's blind spot

> Freud neglects the parents' unconscious completely; he particularly fails to include that precise element into his theoretical framework which would lend it its value, namely the primal seduction.
>
> —Jean Laplanche, 1986, p. 217
> (Translated for this edition)

The banishment of the parental activities from the aetiology of neuroses started with the rejection of the seduction theory and continued in the course of the development of the Oedipus complex. This exiling seems justified in both cases not for logical, but for psychological reasons.

This idea lies in the tradition of Balmary (1982), Krüll (1979) and Kupfersmid (1993) who assume that neither Freud's published nor his unpublished arguments were relevant but rather that psychical reasons were responsible for his rejecting the seduction theory. Kupfersmid (1993), for instance, referring to Freud's statement that "my own father was one of these perverts and is responsible for the hysteria of my brother ... and those of several younger sisters" (letter to Flies, 11 February 1897, 1985c, pp. 230f.), argues that one reason for

41

his renouncement might have been that Freud, to uphold his seduction theory, would have had to conclude that his father's behaviour was suspect. By giving up the seduction theory in favour of the Oedipus complex, the parents were not culprits. It was no longer the parent who seduced the child, but the child who wished to seduce the parent.

In passing, we would like to briefly mention Masson's (1984) assertion that Freud abandoned his seduction theory because of his great desire to be accepted by the Viennese medical establishment. Admittedly, according to Freud, his lecture on the aetiology of hysteria at the psychiatric society "was given an icy reception" and that Krafft-Ebing had rated Freud's thesis ambiguously as "a scientific fairy tale" (letter to Fliess, 26 April 1896, Freud, 1985c, p. 184). However, it is also true that the lecture in which Freud informed his medical colleagues about his thesis was published in the same year in the *Wiener klinischen Rundschau* and that Krafft-Ebing went on to actively support Freud's application for professorship (ibid., p. 229). In discussing Freud's application Krafft-Ebing alluded favourably to Freud's works—among them "On the psychical mechanisms of hysterical phenomena", "The aetiology of hysteria", "The neuro-psychosis of defence", "Obsessions and phobias", "On the grounds for detaching a particular syndrome from neurasthenia under the description 'anxiety neurosis'", "A reply to criticisms of my paper on anxiety neurosis", "Further remarks on the neuro-psychosis of defence". He stated on 10 May 1897:

> The novelty of this research and the difficulty of verifying does not allow us, at this point, to judge its importance with certainty. It is possible that Freud overestimates it and that he generalizes the results he obtained to far ... In any event, his research in this field gives proof of unusual talent and of an ability to guide scientific investigations in new directions. (Gicklhorn & Gicklhorn, 1960, pp. 96f.; translated for this edition)

Apart from the notion that assuming sexual abuse in childhood as the cause for hysteria apparently did not damage Freud's scientific reputation seriously, this is not in line with Masson's assertion that throughout his life, Freud did not hesitate to promote ideas in his field that were not shared by the majority of his medical colleagues.[1]

Even if Masson's thesis were true, it is obvious that it does not exclude internal conflicts on Freud's part. In any event, there are some issues that do indeed substantiate the idea that Freud's turn to phylo-gensis was caused by the intention to portray himself and his parents as innocent participants in the oedipal situation. Gay (1988, p. 505) for instance emphasises that Freud exiled mothers to the margins of his case histories, and Raphael-Leff (1990, p. 325) remarks that Freud's aim was to present the mother "as the unwitting target of her son's lust". This corresponds with his never mentioning mothers as practi-cal seductresses at the time when he still believed in his seduction theory and that he considered his nanny Monika Zajic, not his mother, as his seductress: "She was my instructress in sexual matters" (letter to Fliess, 4 October 1897, 1985c, p. 269), "the prime originator" (letter to Fliess, 3 October 1897, 1985c, p. 268) of "[m]y little hysteria" (letter to Fliess, 14 August 1897, 1985c, p. 261). Freud's glorification of the rela-tionship between son and mother is on the same lines. Freud writes:

> I have found that people who know that they are preferred or favoured by their mother give evidence in their lives of a pecu-liar self-reliance and an unbreakable optimism which often seem like heroic attributes and bring actual success to their possessors. (Freud, 1900a, p. 398)

Some years later he refers to Goethe stressing the same point:

> If a man has been his mother's undisputed darling he retains through-out life the triumphant feeling, the confidence in success, which not seldom brings actual success along with it. (1917b, p. 156)

In 1933, he repeats this position by stating that the relationship between son and mother "is altogether the most perfect, the most free from ambivalence of all human relationships" (1933a, p. 133).

On the other hand, Freud had an "attack of indigestion" every Sunday morning when visiting his mother as long as she lived (Jones, 1955, p. 436; Krüll, 1979, p. 178; Roazen, 1976, p. 65). Wirth (2007) in referring to Krüll (1979), points out that the idealisation of the mother-son relationship serves to disavow the less pleasant side of this relation-ship. Thus Freud writes:

> A mother can transfer to her son the ambition which she has been obliged to suppress in herself, and she can expect from him the

satisfaction of all that has been left over in her of her masculinity complex. Even a marriage is not made secure until the wife has succeeded in making her husband her child as well and in acting as a mother to him. (1933a, pp. 133f.)

Wirth (2007, p. 8) concludes that Freud not only declares that he was emotionally exploited by his mother but also that it is the mother "who forces the son and even the husband into an infantile, incestuous and oedipal role with her unsatisfied ambitions." In this context, Freud's reaction to his mother's death is instructive. On 15 September 1930, three days after his mother's death, he writes to Ernest Jones:

> I will not disguise the fact that my reaction to this event has because of special circumstances been a curious one. Assuredly, there is no saying, what effects such an experience may produce in deeper layers, but on the surface I can detect only two things: an increase in personal freedom, since it was always a terrifying thought that she might come to hear of my death; and secondly, the satisfaction that at last she has achieved the deliverance for which she had earned a right after such a long life. No grief otherwise, such as my ten years younger brother is painfully experiencing. I was not at the funeral; again Anna represented me as at Frankfurt. (Jones, 1957, p. 182)

One day later he repeats this in a letter to Ferenczi:

> It has affected me in a peculiar way, this great event. No pain, no grief, which probably can be explained by the special circumstances—her great age, my pity for her helplessness toward the end; at the same time a feeling of liberation, of release, which I think I also understand. I was not free to die as long as she was alive, and now I am. The values of life will somehow have changed noticeably in the deeper layers. (Freud, 1992g, Vol. III/2, p. 400)

Wirth (2007), takes his words, "it was always a terrifying thought that she might come to hear of my death" to be understood as being freed, having no pain and no grief, and understands them as a slightly twisted death wish towards his mother. This dark side in the relationship to his mother which Freud could not or did not want to admit to himself could explain why Freud portrayed mothers generally as being innocent of partaking in the oedipal events. In freeing the mothers from any guilt he protected them against his aggressions.

After rejecting the seduction theory, Freud also ignored the pathology of fathers in his case histories (Gill, 1987; Ross, 1982), and as Schimek (1987) points out, before he ceded his seduction theory, fathers did not appear as seducers in Freud's published writings. His only references to these were two footnotes in 1924 (Freud, 1895d, p. 134; p. 170), confessing that in the cases of "Katharina" and "Elisabeth v. R." he disguised their fathers as uncles. With his remark "that the old man plays no active part in my case", Freud (letter to Fliess, 3 October 1897, 1985c, p. 268) declared his own father not guilty in relation to himself.

This statement was preceded by a short dream Freud had on the night after his father's funeral and which, in our opinion, indicates the psychological reasons that may have caused Freud to abandon his seduction theory. He reported it to Fliess in the letter from 2 November 1896 (Freud, 1985c, p. 202): "I was in a place where I read a sign: 'You are requested to close the eyes'." He informs Fliess that he recognised the location as the barbershop he visited every day and that on the day of the funeral he was kept waiting and therefore arrived a little late at the house of mourning. He pointed out that in this dream he was in need of leniency for three reasons: First, because he had arranged for the funeral to be quiet and simple—with which his family was initially displeased but later agreed was justified—, second, because he arrived late at the house of mourning, which was also criticised by his family and thirdly because he neglected to do his duty to the dead, in that he had to close his father's eyes (e.g., Krüll, 1979, p. 76). He thought the dream could be an "apology as though I had not done it and were in need of leniency" (Freud, 1985c, p. 202).

In *The Interpretation of Dreams*, this dream occurred the day before his father's funeral and appeared in a slightly different form (1900a, p. 317): "'You are requested to close the eyes' or, 'You are requested to close an eye'." Freud also interprets that "one of the versions: 'You are requested to close an eye'" implies that he needed "to 'wink at' or 'overlook'" something. Yet this leniency only relates to the "puritanical simplicity" in which he had arranged his father's funeral to which members of the family were not sympathetic because they thought that they would "be disgraced in the eyes of those who attended the funeral" (ibid., p. 318). He no longer mentions that he arrived too late at the funeral and that his family agreed with the simplicity of the funeral at a later date.

Their agreement now undergoes the change into the supposition that his father would have agreed with the ceremony's simplicity.

In Krüll's view (1979, pp. 74f.) these changes in detail suggest that this dream expresses a guilt feeling towards his father that Freud presents but tries to hide. Whereas in the first version this guilt feeling appears scenically—Freud arrives too late at his father's funeral and has not done his duty to the dead—, it is absent in the second version. On account of the changed date of the dream's occurrence his late arrival does not have to be mentioned and the leniency the dream asks for relates only to the simplicity of the funeral ceremony. Whereas in the first version Freud loses his guilt towards members of his family—they agreed at a later date with his preference of a simple arrangement—, it seems as if Freud tries to cover up his guilt towards his father by substituting the agreement of his family and by assuming that his father would have agreed on the simplicity of the funeral. In the context presented, this belief appears to be an attempt to prevent concluding that he had a culpable involvement with his father which the first version of the dream would have admitted. In any event, there is no longer any mention of the leniency that he himself is in need of in view of the unsatisfactory fulfilment of this duty towards his father.

Bloch (1989, p. 189; see also Eastman, 2005; Greenberg, 2003; Kupfersmid, 1993), is also not convinced by Freud's interpretation. He considers Freud's (1985c, p. 202; see also 1900a, p. XXVI) statement that "the whole past has been reawakened" and that he felt "quite uprooted" by the death of his father and concludes that in this dream, Freud's conscience demands that he close his eyes to some aspects of his father, to be lenient to him, that is, not to analyse the causal role of fathers (including his own) in the aetiology of neurosis any further. At the time when the dream occurred, Freud was convinced that in the case of hysteria, fathers were guilty of seducing their children (see the letters to Fliess of 6 December 1896 (Freud, 1985c, p. 212), 11 February 1897 (ibid., pp. 231f.), 28 April 1897 (ibid., p. 237), 12 December 1897 (ibid., p. 286) and 22 December (ibid., p. 288).

This interpretation is consistent with the fact that after November 1896, in the letters to Fliess from 8 February 1897 (Freud, 1985c, p. 230), 11 February 1897 (ibid., p. 231), 28 April 1897 (ibid., p. 237) and 14 August 1897 (ibid., p. 261), first doubts appear regarding seduction as the cause of neurotic diseases. Freud's firm statement at a later date, namely that the reports of "almost all my women patients … that they had been seduced by their father ... were untrue" (1933a, p. 120), is, according to Bergmann (1993) and Krüll (1979, p. 95), also less justified by material arguments but rather a result of Freud's changed interest to exonerate fathers.

This change of interest is apparent in his own oedipal situation. In his understanding of this situation, fathers (and mothers) are innocent. In search of Freud's reasons for disregarding the paternal behavioural aspects he had described, Balmary (1982, p. 27) argues: "When someone thus omits part of the story, it is because the omitted section resembles some repressed elements of his personal life." Anzieu (1986, p. 195), Balmary (1982, p. 131), Bernstein (2001), Ross (1982) and Steiner (1994) argue that Freud had identified himself with the Oedipus of Sophocles' version of the Oedipus myth, an identification that led to the conviction that "'I alone am the guilty one'" (Balmary, 1982, p. 131).

This attitude might explain why Freud not only leaves aside all those aspects of the Oedipus myths which refer to an active participation of parental figures in the oedipal drama, but also makes no mention of the incestuous intentions of parents obvious in the other myths with which he was most likely familiar. Both the first edition, published in 1912, and the second, revised edition, published in 1926 of Rank's book *The Incest Theme in Literature and Legend* was in Freud's library (Davies & Fichtner, 2006), and Freud recommended this book several times (e.g., Freud, 1900a, p. 256, footnote added in 1914; letter to Binswanger, 14 June 1912, 1992a, p. 91; 1914d, p. 429; 1916–1917a, p. 337; 1925d, p. 64). We have taken the myths from the edition of this book, published in 1926, all of which were included in the first edition. The majority of these show that the violence of the sons against their fathers is a response to the violence of the fathers against their sons, and that it is not the sons and daughters who approach their parents with incestuous intentions, but parents who approach their children with their incestuous wishes. Considering that Freud was well acquainted with the fact "that the myths of every people, and not only of the Greeks, are filled with examples of love-affairs between fathers and daughters and even between mothers and sons (1926e, p. 214), yet only focuses on Sophocles' *Oedipus Tyrannus* in which Oedipus blames himself alone for what happens, it is very likely that Freud's active exclusion and his focus on *Oedipus Tyrannus* can much less be put down to logical than to psychological reasons.

Along with Freeman (1967) it seems to us that the guilt Freud must have experienced—in Sophocles drama it is followed by blinding which Freud (1912–1913a, p. 130) understands as "castration"— was probably the reason why he was attracted to Darwin's theory of the primal horde.

This conception offered the possibility of decreasing his own guilt in the oedipal event by projecting it on to his imagined parricidal forerunner similar to the way that he assumed it effective prehistorically. Here the brothers project their guilt for murdering the primal father on to one of themselves. One of them becomes "the Hero of the great primeval tragedy" (1912–1913a, p. 156) because he bears the guilt of the others on his shoulders and relieves the other brothers from their guilt. It is in this sense that Freud interprets the relation between Oedipus and choir in Sophocles' *Oedipus Tyrannus*. He understands this relation as a re-enactment of "primeval tragedy", whereby

> the tragic guilt was the guilt which he [the Hero] had to take on himself in order to relieve the Chorus from theirs ... The crime which was thrown on to his shoulders ... was precisely the crime for which the members of the Chorus, the company of brothers, were responsible. (Freud, 1912–1913a, p. 156; see also 1939a, p. 87)

As is the case with Freud Balmary's (1982, p. 131) statement "'I alone am the guilty one'" applies also to that Hero.

Several statements support the idea that Freud projected his feelings of guilt onto the anonymous Hero in a way that was similar to the company of brothers whereby the Hero alone became responsible for the murder of the primal father. Considering that by his identification with Oedipus, his own guilt appeared in the guise of the Hero's "tragic guilt" in consciousness, it is to be assumed that it was really his own feeling of guilt that Freud struggled with while giving birth to *Totem and Taboo* (e.g., Bonomi, 1996, p. 180; Kramer, 1995, p. 301), and which he revealed to Ferenczi in a letter, dated 21 May 1911 (Freud, 1992g, Vol. 1, p. 281): "I am tormented by the secret of tragic guilt". Six months later he deciphered it as the outcome of projections of the company of brothers. After informing Jones of his intense inner pressure while working on *Totem and Taboo*—"There are a great many things boiling in my head" (letter to Jones, dated 5 November 1911, cited in Jones, 1955, p. 351)—, he tells Ferenczi that he has the outcome of his work already in his head: "The work on totem is a mess. I am reading fat books without any real interest, since *I know the conclusions already; my instinct tells me so"* (letter to Ferenczi, dated 30 November 1911; Freud, 1992g, Vol. 1, p. 316; our italics). If the results were there after six months work, the question arises as to why the whole work was not finished. The work had to be continued because—as Freud (ibid, p. 317) states in the above citation—"all the material has to be ground through".

Although this addendum can be interpreted differently, in our view it also allows us to assume that Freud was looking for convincing examples to validate his projection thesis. We cannot reject the idea that it is also for this reason that Freud uses the religion of Mithras and Christianity in particular (Freud, 1912–1913a, p. 153), and it is surely indisputable that such a validation of the manifest content of his thesis is particularly necessary if this content is also used in the service of concealing its latent content—in this case the projection of his own guilt.

Since the action of closing one eye means being lenient with what one still sees with the other eye, assuming that there is such a dynamic, it is understandable that in contrast to other writings—such as *The Interpretation of Dreams*—Freud's attitude toward his phylogenetic considerations is contradictory. On the one hand, he seems to be convinced of the scientific validity of the thesis he presented in *Totem and Taboo* and in *Moses and Monotheism*. For instance, when working on the fourth chapter of *Totem and Taboo* he writes on 4 May 1913 to Ferenczi that it was his "greatest, best, and perhaps my last good thing. Inner certainties tell me that I am right" (Freud, 1992g, p. 481). This he repeats four days later: "I haven't written anything with so much conviction since the *Interpretation of Dreams*" (ibid., p. 482), and on 13 May 1913, when the work on *Totem and Taboo* was finished, he writes to him again stating that "not since the *Interpretation of Dreams* have I worked on anything with the same feeling of certainty and elation" (ibid., pp. 485f.). Furthermore, when Jones' (1957, p. 313) asks him "to alter ... a sentence ... in the Moses book in which he expressed the Lamarckian view in universal terms ... since no responsible biologist regarded it as tenable any longer", Freud answers: "[T]hey were all wrong and the passage must stay". In 1939 (1939a, p. 100) he stresses that in contradistinction to the present attitude of biological sciences he still cannot do without the assumption "of the inheritance of acquired characters by succeeding generations".

On the other hand, as early as 14 January 1912 Freud states in a letter to Abraham (Freud, 1965a, p. 147) that he doesn't think that his work is good, and four weeks after he reported his feeling of certainty he writes to Ferenczi on 12 June 1913: "I have retreated far from my initial high opinion of the work and am, on the whole, dubious about it" (1992g, p. 491), and in the letter, dated 17 June 1913, he repeats: "The work on totem has still not fully come up to my expectations. It is too uncertain" (ibid., p. 492). In addition, Freud (1921c, p. 122) considers the ideas expressed in *Totem and Taboo* not as sound knowledge, but as "only a hypothesis, like so many others with which archaeologists endeavour to lighten the darkness of prehistoric times", as a "'just so story'" (Freud, 1921c, p. 122), as a "scientific myth" (ibid., p. 135), or as a "scientific fantasy" standing "not at the end, but rather at the beginning of an understanding of this phylogenetic factor" (1985a, p. 20). It is also true that Freud gave the first version of the study of *Moses* the subtitle "A historical novel" (Yerushalmi, 1989, p. 375), and in a letter to Max Eitington, dated 27 November 1934, he writes about his work on *Moses*, which he first did not want to publish: "Experts would find it easy to discredit me as an outsider" (cited in Jones, 1957, p. 194). He was not satisfied with the historical part in particular. In a letter to Arnold Zweig, dated 11 November 1934, he writes that

> this historical novel won't stand up to my own criticism. I need more certainty and I should not like to endanger the final formula of the whole book, which I regard as valuable, by founding it on a base of clay. So we will put it aside. (cited in Jones, 1957, p. 194)

Our explanation of Freud's transfer of the Oedipus complex from ontogenesis into phylogenesis is, indisputably, no more than a supposition. Possibly we are correct, but it is not the only conceivable explanation. However, it is remarkable how smoothly our individual psychological explanation fits in with the social psychological views Devereux (1953) puts forward in answer to the question why Freud reduces parental behaviour to some sort of unspecific external trigger and misses the opportunity, as Laplanche (1986, p. 217) remarks in the quotation at the beginning of this chapter, of embedding the parents' unconscious into the aetiopathogenesis of neuroses in a systematic fashion. Devereux refers to

> the adult's deep-seated need to place all responsibility for the Oedipus complex upon the child, and to ignore, whenever possible, certain parental attitudes which actually stimulate the infant's oedipal tendencies. (Devereux, 1953, p. 132)

CHAPTER EIGHT

Oedipus myths and the Oedipus complex

> The Oedipus Complex in particular, in terms of which Freud understood the Oedipus myth, has been reapplied to this and to other Greek myths hundreds of times. The procedure can, however, be reversed, and the Oedipus myth can be used to analyze the Oedipus Complex.
>
> —Lowell Edmunds, 1985, p. 87

If we insert those aspects of Oedipus myths that Freud excludes into the Oedipus complex, it comes to light that the son's rivalry with his father and the rivalry between the daughter and her mother—from Freud's point of view the starting point of the Oedipus complex—both stem from a projective identification on the part of the father and of the mother respectively (e.g., Mann, 1993, see also Bick, 1989; Ross, 1982; Young, 1988). We shall begin with the Oedipus complex of the boy.

The oedipal drama of the male

It is common knowledge that in Freud's conception the son competes with the father for the mother. The father threatens his son with castration, and the son identifies with the aggressor, the father (e.g., Freud, 1923b, pp. 32ff.).

However, because Freud excluded those aspects of the Oedipus myth that refer to the activities of the parents, he was blind to the fact that the oedipal rivalry he describes is not staged by the son, but by the father, and that the son's identification with the father is preceded by the father's projective identification. He also ignores the fact that in many myths the mother prefers the son to the father. In so doing, the mother reactivates the father's oedipal drama by way of which the son becomes the father's rival. As long as the mother has a preference for him, the son has no reason to compete with his father in his relationship with the mother.

The father's projective identification changes the situation. The father projects his own aggressions, stemming from his rivalry with his son, onto his son, and his son identifies with this projected aggression, thus enabling himself to avert the danger ensuing from his father's aggression. In this way the son returns his father's aggression and begins to compete with him. Freud's thesis that the oedipal rivalry begins with the son constitutes in a mystified form the father's rivalry with his son.

Similarly, Freud ignores the references the myths make to the negative Oedipus complex, as for instance in the myth, in which Laius has a homosexual relationship with Chrysippus (Constans, 1881, p. 26; Devereux, 1953; Graves, 1955, p. 403; Gruppe, 1906a, p. 520; Mann, 1993; Pollock, 1986; Roscher, 1884–1890, p. 903; Ross, 1982). "Paedophilia", as Licht (1912, p. 441) stated, "was to the Greeks at first the most important way of bringing up the male youth", and two myths, in one of which Laius is seen as the "'father' of pederasty" (Pollock, 1986, p. 79; see also Devereux, 1953; Mann, 1993) and in the other as starting the swordfight with Oedipus at the three-way intersection, refer relatively openly to the homosexuality that undermines the love of the father for his son.

Devereux stated:

> Chrysippus is, in a sense, the representative of Oedipus' own passive homosexual characteristics, which were brought into being, or were at least aroused, by Laius' aggressive and homosexual impulses towards his son. (Devereux, 1953, p. 134)

If we regard Chrysippus and Oedipus as one person, we may be justified in assuming that these myths point to the father's love for his son and relate them to the negative Oedipus complex. As a child, his mother competed with him for the love of his father; the son identified with his rival, his mother, and took his father (or himself) as his love object (Freud, 1905d, p. 145; 1910c, p. 100; 1923b, p. 33). On the basis of his own negative Oedipus complex and in repeating the past, the father now chooses his own son as his love object (e.g., Ceccarelli, 2003) and competes with his son's mother for his love.

Freud's idea is that the Oedipus complex is usually "twofold, positive and negative" (Freud, 1923b, p. 33). Devereux (1953, p. 132) summarised the togetherness of both the positive and negative Oedipus complexes of the father as the "Laius complex". The mythological version, in which Laius is scared by a dream and leaves Thebes to inquire about the fate of the exposed Oedipus (Roscher, 1897–1909, p. 713; Schneiderhan, 1852, p. 20), whereby the myth does not inform us whether Laius wishes to convince himself that Oedipus is dead or whether he hopes that Oedipus is alive (Robert, 1915, p. 97), relates to both of these complexes.

Both complexes are also pictured in the myths in which Laius rapes Chrysippus, exposes Oedipus and pierces his ankles with an iron nail. All of these actions symbolically portray the violence, that is, castration, born out of the positive Oedipus complex and the homosexual love resulting from the negative Oedipus complex (Devereux, 1960). The swollen foot resulting from piercing the ankles indicates most clearly that a penis is required on the love object. The swollen foot is comparable to an erect penis (Ferenczi, 1912, p. 15; letter to C. G. Jung, dated 21 November 1909, Freud, 1974a, p. 266), expressing the father's admiration for the genitals of his son. The fact that Oedipus has not just one but two swollen feet might also point to the positive and negative Oedipus complex. Both might symbolise that Oedipus is the object of heterosexual as well as homosexual actions, both requiring an erect penis.

It is evident that the myths referring to the negative Oedipus complex contradict the castrating tendency that can be seen in the myths relating to the positive Oedipus complex of the father. The tendency contradicting castration can also be found in the myth in which Laius does not kill his son himself but entrusts Jocasta with Oedipus' exposure, likely because "his homosexual love for his son was too strong for him" (Stewart, 1961, p. 426; see also Mann, 1993).

The oedipal drama of the female

Before comparing these mythological issues with Freud's female Oedipus complex, we will first examine the Oedipus complex that mothers generally undergo. In Freud's conception, their positive

Oedipus complex "is made possible and led up to by the castration complex" (Freud, 1925j, p. 256; italics omitted). The girl discovers that she has no penis and blames her mother for the condition in which "a castration … has been carried out" (ibid., p. 257). The girl "gives up her wish for a penis and puts in place of it a wish for a child: and with that purpose in view she takes her father as a love-object. Her mother becomes the object of her jealousy" (ibid., p. 256). This rivalry finally leads to an "identification with her mother" (1939a, p. 125).

Freud contended that the daughter's penis envy stems from her anatomy and this causes her to compete with her mother. Much has been written about penis envy since then (for an overview, see, e.g., Dahl, 1996; Lax, 1995; 2007; Moulton, 1970) and we will not discuss these various interpretations, but simply confront the Freudian understanding with the notions that can be inferred from mythology.

Mythology offers us another reason to explain why the daughter turns towards the father. The incest of Menoeceus and Jocasta informs us that a father's sexual interest in his daughter may be similar to the one he has for his wife. The myths also show that fathers prefer their daughter as a younger version of her mother. For example Thebaldo, Prince of Salern, promises his dying wife that he would only take the woman who was able to wear her wedding ring. Thebaldo knew that this ring would only fit the finger of Doralice, his daughter that he was in love with (Rank, 1926, p. 319). In the story of the beautiful Sesselja, the king, her father, mourned for a long time over the death of his queen and declared that he would only marry a young maiden who was as beautiful as his dead wife. One day he saw his young daughter Sesselja dressed up in her mother's best clothing and as she was more beautiful than her mother he wanted to marry her (Riklin & White, 1915).

Freud also commented on the "usual sexual attraction" that "had drawn together the father and daughter" (1905e. p. 21; see also 1900a, p. 258; 1910a, p. 47; 1916–1917a, p. 207, p. 333). When he writes that "the affections of the little girl are fixed on her father, who has probably done all he could to win her love" (1919e, p. 186),[1] he is emphasising the father's seductive role and its intensity which evoke the girl's incestuous wishes towards him. Likewise, he is familiar with the envy of the mother aroused by the sexual attraction between father and daughter. The mother, he states, "is warned by her daughter's growth that the time has come when she herself must abandon her claims to sexual satisfaction" (1900a, p. 257), and he held that a girl may suffer "from her mother's jealousy owing to the preference shown her by her father" (1900a, p. 363).

However, in his conception of the female Oedipus complex he ignores the significance of the father's sexually charged advances that cause the daughter to become a rival to her mother. The incest in the myths suggests that the daughter challenges the mother for the sole possession of the father's penis. Lorand (1939, p. 438) stated this issue more than seventy years ago, "The child feels weak and small compared to the mother, and the penis envy refers to the father's penis ... of which the mother was the sole recipient". However, as the father prefers his daughter, she initially has no reason to compete with her mother. The mother does not become her rival until after the daughter has identified with the aggressive wishes initiated by the mother's rivalry being projected onto her daughter. Just as the son identifies with the aggressions projected onto him by his father to avert their danger, the daughter also identifies herself for the same reason with the aggressive wishes her mother has projected onto her.

In the same way as the father, who after his projective identification registers his rivalry with his son as his son's competition with him, the mother, on account of her projective identification, also perceives her own rivalry as her daughter's competition with her. This rivalry strongly suggests that by emphasising her motherhood to her daughter, the mother intends unconsciously to convince her that she alone has possession of the father's penis.

To the daughter, motherhood reveals to her why her father only offers his penis to the mother. From the daughter's point of view the one who has a child has the father's penis at her disposal. Consequently, the daughter wishes to become a mother and to take her mother's place. Thus, she identifies with her mother and makes advances to her father with hopes of receiving a child that would symbolise her possession of the father's penis.[2]

It is the father's penis which the mother withholds from her daughter that clothes itself in anatomical garment in Freud's formulation "that in the end the girl's mother, who sent her into the world so insufficiently equipped, is almost always held responsible for her lack of a penis" (Freud, 1925j, p. 254). When the daughter gives birth to a child later in life, she fulfils her unconscious desire to have a child by her father. In Jocasta's case, it appears that the meanings of father and child are condensed in the person Oedipus. He is simultaneously both the father (of her children) and her son.

The myths suggest a modification of Abraham's (1920, p. 10) *"wish-fulfilment type"*. In Abraham's view, this type of person believes unconsciously that it has a penis, but when seen from the perspective of the myths, the "wish-fulfilment type" does not desire such an organ but needs to employ the father's penis as means of fulfilling her wish for a child. From a mythological viewpoint, the *"wish-fulfilment type"* (Abraham, 1920, p. 10) seems to be an elaboration of the mother's positive Oedipus complex. Thus, in the formula, "I shall receive the 'gift' one day" (ibid., p. 12), the gift does not refer to a penis but to a child.

In the mythological presentations of Jocasta, there are also behaviours that are congruent with the *"revenge type"* (ibid., p. 10). Jocasta can only seduce Laius to beget children when he is in a drunken state (Devereux, 1953; Gruppe, 1906a, p. 520; Graves, 1955, p. 371; Pollock, 1986; Roscher, 1897–1909, p. 703; Stewart, 1961; Stimmel, 2004) and in Abraham's (1920, p. 20) revenge type, "there exists a wish to get a child from a man against his will".

The revenge type can be understood as an elaboration of the negative Oedipus complex. In the negative Oedipus complex the girl's father competes with her for the love of the mother and threatens his daughter with the loss of his love. To avoid this risk of paternal love loss, the daughter identifies with her paternal rival. This identification is also motivated by a desire to compensate for the advantage her rival has. In the eyes of the daughter, he has that attribute which presupposes the mother as a condition of her love. By means of this identification, the daughter equips herself unconsciously with a penis, so that she can present herself to her mother as a love object, which in its crucial detail is just like the father (see Burstein & Gillian, 1997).

Being merely similar to the rival is not sufficient. To become the single love object of the mother an exclusive feature is needed, and this seems to be that attempt from which later in life the castrating tendencies of this type arises. If we apply to the daughter the same results that Freud describes for the negative Oedipus complex of the son—he takes, as mentioned, himself or his father for his love object—, her later love object has to have, in contrast to that of the son, no penis, regardless of whether it represents the mother and/or the daughter herself. Therefore, if the daughter's later love object is of heterosexual nature, there will be castrating tendencies towards this object.

Once the anatomically determined penis envy has been rejected, the "desire to take by force the longed-for organ, i.e., to rob the man of it" (Abraham, 1920, p. 16) should no longer be understood as "longing for revenge on the man." The unconscious tendency "to take the penis from the man" (ibid., p. 20) no longer serves to acquire father's penis. It serves as a means to remove the rival and/or to feminise the future love object.

Even if there are no mythological findings supporting the idea of a negative Oedipus complex of Jocasta, it seems appropriate to rename Abraham's *revenge type* into *castration type*. Certainly, Jocasta's repetition of the incest with her father, Menoeceus (Stewart, 1961), and his suicide (Graves, 1955, p. 373; Stimmel, 2004) suggest that she identified with her father, as would be indicative of a negative Oedipus complex. However, in the case of sexual abuse, we can justify the identification with Menoeceus by the idea that victims of sexual abuse tend to identify with the offender (see Zepf & Zepf, 2008).

On the assumption that Abraham's "revenge type" is synonymous with "castration type", the mythology supports Abraham's (1920, p. 78) supposition that both types are connected. De Saussure (1920, p. 118; see also Devereux, 1953) subsumed both types under the term *"Complexe de Jocaste"*. In Euripides' (Edmunds, 1985) and Sophocles' versions of the Oedipus drama, Jocasta is actively involved in the exposure of Oedipus. Jocasta's castrating inclination divulges itself by her exposing Oedipus, and her opposite tendency is portrayed when in the myth, like Laius, Jocasta does not personally kill her son but gives him to a servant and

> presumably, not wishing her son, for whom she had longed so much, to die, intimated to him by gesture, tone of voice, or possibly directly in words, that the baby should not be left to die. (Stewart, 1961, p. 426)

The myths also underscore that the wish to have children and the castration wish can be regarded as reciprocal use as a means to an end. In the case of the seduction of the drunken Laius, Jocasta takes over Laius' genitals, robbing him of his penis, so to speak, and uses this castration as a means of fulfilling her wish for children. We find the same relationship when Oedipus' ankles are pierced and the feet become swollen. We note Jocasta's castrating tendency in her piercing the ankles (e.g., Rank, 1926, p. 218), and Jocasta's admiration of her son's genital potency is displayed by the emerging swollen feet derived from this piercing. The genital potency of Jocasta's son is also expressed by another mythological version that states that Oedipus fathered four children in one action (Roscher, 1897–1909, p. 728). In other mythological scenes, Jocasta uses the fulfilled wish for children as a means to castrate the father. It is claimed that Jocasta was present when Oedipus and Laius were fighting (ibid., p. 711, p. 731), she recognised and favoured her son, observed her son murder her husband and then seduced her son following the murder (Devereux, 1953; Gruppe, 1906a, p. 524; Rank, 1926, p. 191, p. 216; Rosenman, 1982). The same issue is also found in the version in which Oedipus recalls his encounter with Laius in the presence of Jocasta, shows her the place where he killed Laius and pres-ents to her the belt (Robert, 1915, p. 508; Schneiderhan, 1852, p. 30) that he had taken from the dead Laius. Although Jocasta recognises Oedipus as the murderer of Laius, she keeps this information to herself (Roscher, 1897–1909, p. 729; Schneiderhan, 1852, p. 30).

CHAPTER NINE

The heterosexual and homosexual processing of the oedipal drama

> Closer study usually discloses the more complete Oedipus complex, which is twofold, positive and negative ... that is to say, a boy has not merely an ambivalent attitude towards his father and an affectionate object-choice towards his mother, but at the same time he also behaves like a girl and displays an affectionate feminine attitude to his father and a corresponding jealousy and hostility towards his mother.
>
> —Sigmund Freud, 1923b, p. 33

Although mythology does not portray the child but the parents as staging the oedipal drama, the mythological versions do not disagree with Freud's assumption that the drama is always twofold in that it includes both heterosexual and homosexual aspects. The mythological versions are consistent with Freud's (1923b, p. 33) assumption that "everyone, even the most normal, is capable of making a homosexual object-choice and has done so at some time in life, and ... still adheres to it in his unconscious" (1910c, p. 99). Furthermore, these versions also provide information about the way the positive and negative Oedipus complexes relate to each other. The negative shaping of the complex does not ward off the positive shaping, as Hornstra (1966) assumed, and the negative shaping is not warded off by its positive shaping. The son does not ward off his love for his mother in order to choose his father as his love object, but does so because the father threatens him with castration. Equally, he does not ward off his love for the father so that he can turn to his mother, but does so because his mother threatens him with the loss of her love.

As the myths show, both forms of the complex are warded off but remain virulent. Freud's (1916–1917a, p. 335) statements that "each of these neurotics has himself been an Oedipus" yet "has, as a reaction to the complex, become a Hamlet", and that "In the *Oedipus* the child's wishful phantasy that underlies it is brought into the open and realised as it would be in a dream. In *Hamlet* it remains repressed" (1900a, p. 264). This applies not only to the heterosexual, but also for the homosexual processing of the drama. Laius and Jocasta do not interact their positive or negative Oedipus complexes with the original objects, but with their substitutes. Both complexes are warded off by building substitutive formations in which the substituted scenes are re-enacted in a mystified manner.

This condensation is indifferent to what kind of love object the son will choose at a later date. Although we do not intend to go deeply into the factors deciding on whether the love object is ultimately heterosexual or homosexual in nature, we would at least like to present a reminder of Freud's views. Referring to the mothers of Sadger's patients, Freud (1910c, p. 99) stated that "the mothers of his homosexual patients were frequently masculine women, women with energetic traits of character, who were able to push the father out of his proper place", and he emphasised:

> I have occasionally seen the same thing, but I was more strongly impressed by cases in which the father was absent from the beginning or left the scene at an early date, so that the boy found himself left entirely under feminine influence. Indeed it almost seems as though the presence of a strong father would ensure that the son made the correct decision in his choice of object, namely someone of the opposite sex. (Freud, 1910c, p. 9)

Allen (1965), Bak (1953), Eigen (1975), and Neubauer (1960) were also convinced that male homosexuality is established by an identification with a phallic mother. In generalising Freud's considerations, one could argue that in the oedipal situation, boys and girls primarily identify with the object that poses the greatest danger, thereby acquiring their gender identity. If a positive Oedipus complex is dominant, individuals choose a person of the opposite sex as a substitute but, unknown to him/her, has aspects of his/her own sex. In the case of a negative Oedipus complex s/he chooses an object of his/her own sex but, unknown to them, has aspects of the individuals' opposite sex.

The myths also inform us that the complete Oedipus complex is not founded on a genetically based bisexuality (Freud, 1923b, p. 33), and that it only presupposes bisexuality as a necessary condition, that is, as a possibility. When parental oedipal problems transmitted over the generations enforce their influence, one of these biological options comes into realisation.

CHAPTER TEN

Unconscious oedipal messages and answers

> Neurotic parents have … neurotic children, and the child's
> Oedipus complex reflects that of his parents.
>
> —Otto Fenichel, 1931, p. 421

Having rejected Freud's idea that in Sophocles' *Oedipus Tyrannus* infantile experiences are correctly portrayed, and having supplemented Freud's Oedipus complex with the aspects that he ignored in Sophocles' drama alongside those that can be found in other myths, we are now witness to the central role of the child in conflicting interests.

Before entering into the debate, we want to point out that the parents not only represent for each other the original objects of their positive Oedipus complex, but also the original objects of their negative one. Furthermore, we shall restrict ourselves to those oedipal problems which end in a heterosexual object choice.

Under these conditions we would like to focus first on the daughter. She is cared for by a mother who loves her both in repetition of her own negative Oedipus complex but also competes with her daughter for the love of the father because of her own positive Oedipus complex. The mother displaces the oedipal relationship to her own mother from the representation of her husband onto the representation of her daughter. This displacement causes the mother to compete unconsciously with her own mother, in the mystified shape of her daughter, for the penis of her father and to compete with her father, in the mystified shape of her husband, for her mother's love.

The myths tell us that, given this scenery, the daughter is confronted with a father for whom she unconsciously represents the original object of his positive Oedipus complex. The father transfers his oedipal relationship to his mother from the representation of his wife onto the representation of his daughter. Since his representation of his wife includes his father as a secret element, being the object of his negative Oedipus complex, when competing with his wife and daughter he is unconsciously competing with his father for his mother's love and with his daughter for his father's love.

One could object that the myths portray the father as being attracted to his daughter mostly after the death of the wife. This can be undoubtedly understood in the way that the father's attraction to his daughter causes him to lose sexual interest in his wife, so that she becomes non-existent for him in this respect. However, at the same time the death of his wife serves as a camouflage for his incestuous desires towards his daughter.

Obviously, the tendencies arising from the parents' positive and negative Oedipus complex force their daughter into an awkward situation. On the manifest level, both parents love their daughter and at the same time compete either with her or for her unconsciously. The mother loves her daughter in her negative Oedipus complex and competes with her in her positive Oedipus complex for the father's love; the father loves his daughter in his positive Oedipus complex and competes with her for his mother's love in his negative Oedipus complex. The mother is jealous of the daughter for her father's affection, the father is jealous of her for her maternal affection.

To understand the daughter's oedipal problem it is crucial that both parents project their oedipal strivings onto their daughter and that the daughter identifies with these projections. The daughter is transformed from being the object of parental strivings into being their subject and the parents become objects of the oedipal strivings of their daughter. The daughter upholds the oedipal problems of her parents, envies the mother the father and the father the mother, and takes over the (unconscious) guilt feelings of her parents. As a reaction to this projective identification with her parents' unconscious wishes the daughter will identify with both of them and consequently choose a love object via an unconscious condensation of aspects of both mother and father.

The son in turn sees himself as the object of his father's "'Laius complex'", understood as "a transfiguration of the adult father's childhood oedipal constellation", and as containing "both filicidal and pederastic trends" (Ross, 1984, p. 395). The son is the object of castration wishes stemming from the father's positive Oedipus complex, but at the same time he is the object of a caring father who, resulting from his negative Oedipus complex, loves his son, a love that presupposes his love object's possession of a penis. The father has transferred the original object of his negative Oedipus complex from the representation of his wife onto the representation of his son, and restages in this framework both his positive and negative Oedipus complex. In the figures of his son and his wife the father competes unconsciously with his father for the love of his mother, thus producing his tendency to castrate his son. In these figures he concurrently competes unconsciously with his own mother for his father's love.

According to the myths, the son faces a mother whose behaviour is determined by the "*Complexe de Jocasta*" (De Saussure, 1920, p. 118; Devereux, 1953). The mother's positive Oedipus complex causes her to love her son and admire his penis but at the same time to desire and rob him of the admired object. The mother displaces the original object of her positive Oedipus complex from the representation of her husband onto the representation of her son, and restages in this constellation both her positive and negative Oedipus complex. In the figures of her husband and her son the mother unconsciously competes with her own mother for the love of her own father and with her own father for the love of her own mother, a love which gave rise to the castrating tendencies towards her son.

Apparently, this tendency arising from the mother's negative Oedipus complex works in a synergistic way with the father's castrating tendency which results from his positive Oedipus complex. Both of these tendencies counteract the aims of the mother's positive Oedipus complex and father's negative Oedipus complex, namely to ensure that the genitals of their son remain intact. It seems that this intention prevents the parents from performing the castration of their son.

Like the daughter, the parents' positive and negative Oedipus complexes afford the son an awkward situation. The son, too, is loved by both. The father loves his son because of his negative Oedipus complex, and he competes with him for the love of his mother because of his positive Oedipus complex; the mother loves her son because of her positive Oedipus complex, and she competes with him for the father because of her negative Oedipus complex. The father envies his son the mother's admiration of his phallicity, thus counteracting his castrating tendencies, and the mother envies her son his father's affection.

If we are to understand the son's oedipal drama it is crucial that both parents project their oedipal strivings onto their son who identifies with these projections, so that in this case, too, object and subject exchanged. The object of the parental strivings is transformed into the subject and the parents become the objects of the oedipal strivings of their son.

Like the daughter, the son reproduces the oedipal drama of his parents, envies the father the mother and the mother the father, and takes on the (unconscious) guilt feelings of his parents. After projective identification with his parents' unconscious wishes, the son identifies with both of them and in the outcome he will later choose a love object via an unconscious condensation of aspects of both mother and father.

If we understand "self-object" in Grotstein's (1978) sense as the product, mediated by projective identification, of transference of aspects belonging to the self-representation into an object representation, (e.g., Joseph, 1988, p. 629), it becomes immediately apparent that with the interchange of subject and object in the oedipal situation children acquire the status of self-objects for their parents. Parents love their child because the child is identified with the parts of the parents they have unconsciously projected onto their child, and because these parts can be subsequently treated by the parents as if they belonged to their child.

In addition, we want to remark that the representation of the later love object can also be condensed with aspects of one's own person. Freud describes this taking the example of homosexual object choice. In this case, the boy

> represses his love for his mother: he puts himself in her place,
> identifies himself with her, and takes his own person as a model in
> whose likeness he chooses the new objects of his love. In this way
> he has become a homosexual ... the boys whom he now loves as
> he grows up are after all only substitutive figures and revivals of
> himself in childhood—boys whom he loves in the way in which

his mother loved him when he was a child. He finds the objects of his love along the path of *narcissism*. (Freud, 1910c, p. 100; see also 1905d, p. 145; 1923b, p. 33)

Alike the projective identification rendering children to be their parents' self-objects, a child's later object choice can be based on such projective identifications even if it is not accompanied by overt homosexuality. In this case, the individual's relationship to his love object is based on condensations not only of aspects of his mother and his father, but also on those with aspects of him/herself. This projective identification on which later object choice is based is preceded by the previous projective identification initiated by the parents on the psyche of their child.

We think it is clear by now that children are trapped in the oedipal triangles of their parents. Both the relationship father-daughter-mother and the relationship mother-son-father repeat the original oedipal constellations of the father and the mother. This explains why "the father will choose his daughter and the mother her son as a favourite" (Freud, 1916–1917a, p. 207), not only when multiple children are present (ibid., pp. 352f.). As the myths show, the mother prefers her son in comparison with his father, and the father his daughter in comparison with her mother. In other words, the father's rivalry with his son, resulting from his positive Oedipus complex, is triggered by the mother, who, in repetition of her Oedipus complex prefers him to his father, and the mother's rivalry with her daughter stemming from the mother's positive Oedipus complex is triggered by the father, who, in repetition of his Oedipus complex prefers her to her mother. The father's envy of his son cannot only be put down to his own psychodynamic situation, but also to the psychodynamic situation of the mother, and the envy the mother has of her daughter is based not alone on her own psychodynamic state, but also on the psychodynamics of the father who prefers his daughter.

CHAPTER ELEVEN

Oedipus Tyrannus—a cover story

> I am sorry to say this, but no-one has understood before now
> that "Oedipus" is not about the revelation of truth but about the
> cover up of truth ... And it has nothing to do with the Oedipus
> Complex because Oedipus never had a complex.
>
> —Hovhannes Pilikian, 1974

Myths leave no doubt that the chain of tragic events in the Oedipus
drama was not initiated by Oedipus the son, but by Laius the
father. It was Laius' fear that caused him to stage the drama with
his son, not Oedipus and his desire. Viewed from the perspective
of the myths, Freud's statement that all individuals are condemned
to undergo the Oedipus complex "because the oracle laid the same
curse upon us before our birth as upon him" (Freud, 1900a, p. 262),
has to be understood in the sense that children are generally destined to be victims of the fear, jealousy, yearnings, and expectations
of their parents.

One might point out that Abraham (1909, p. 269) considered myths as
dreams. As dreams they represent unconscious wishes as fulfilled and
one could argue that the portrayal of the oedipal drama in the myths
is a wish-fulfilment, because in reality the situation is reversed and the

69

children are freed from any guilt by their presentation as victims and the parents are identified as the perpetrators.

However, this objection is not valid, myths are not dreams. They are formed on the basis of dreams (e.g., Rank, 1913), and in Freud's view, infantile wishes in dreams are not represented as fulfilled. In his view, "the dream may aptly be characterised as an *attempt* at the fulfilment of a wish" (Freud, 1925d, p. 46). Myths are "childhood memories that a nation preserves" (1901b, p. 48). They "testify to the upheaval in the child's emotional life" (1908c, p. 217), and do not primarily pertain to a wish-fulfilment or to an attempt at wish-fulfilment.

But even if the myths did represent a wish-fulfilment, one would have to clarify the basis on which the child would develop its incestuous and aggressive fantasies. As these fantasies can no longer be attributed to an archaic inheritance and as they consist solely of "material which has been acquired" from "a reality experienced by the child" (1918b, p. 55), there is no good reason to assume that the child is the sole author of oedipal fantasies and that in these myths, the authorship of these fantasies is attributed to the parents with the intention of keeping the child blameless. The myths rather suggest that in building its incestuous and aggressive fantasies, the child "usually follows some indication from its parents, whose affection bears the clearest characteristics of a sexual activity, even though of one that is inhibited in its aims" (1910a, p. 47). As Bick (1989), Mann (1993), and Young (1988) assert, this suggestion consists of a projection of the parents' incestuous and aggressive wishes and the child's identification with these parental projections. We must stress the fact that Freud's (e.g., 1921c, pp. 105f.) description of the identification with the parents, as A. Rascovsky and M. Rascovsky (1972) have also emphasised, is preceded by a projective identification initiated by the parents.

How in the myths "reality .... is experienced by the child" (1918b, p. 55) depends on the degree of defence demanded (Rank, 1926, p. 27), that is to say, depends on what a culture can tolerate (Devereux, 1956, p. 12). Sophocles' *Oedipus Tyrannus* is due to an identification with the parental projections and the camouflage of warded off aspects, whilst in the other myths the scenery existing before such an identification is portrayed more or less obviously. For instance, the incestuous intentions of the mother are portrayed more openly in the stories surrounding Agrippina and Nero, Semiramis and her son, Periander and his mother. They appear mystified in the guise of the Empress and widow seduced by the devil and in the legends of Judas and Cyborea, Salchâ and her son, the latter mystified as fate. The father's incestuous intentions are pictured more openly in the legends of Zeus and Persephone, they are mystified as sheer fate in the legend of Clymenus and Harpalyce and in oral form in the Cypriot tale, and in the myth of Antiochus and his daughter they are masked by the dying wife's recommendation and the protection taken to prevent the daughter from having sexual interaction with other men. This kind of camouflage also applies to the Armenian saga of the priest's daughter Assily.

The father's murderous impulses are evident in the myths of Uranus and Cronus, in the myths of Tantalus and Pelops they are disguised by way of testing the cognitive ability of the Gods, in the tale of Aun and Odin the securing of one's own survival blurs them, in the myth of Jörmurek and Randvew it is the intrigue of Bikki, in the myth of Cuchulainn and Conloch it is the ignorance of the father, in the saga of sun and stars it is the astrological form, and in the relationship between God and Jesus the murderous impulses are obscured by the belief that Jesus dies to take away the sins of the world.

We can hardly overlook the fact that the myths' reading of Sophocles' *Oedipus Tyrannus* corresponds partially to Freud's phylogenetic justification of the Oedipus complex. In Freud's concept of a primal horde, the "violent and jealous father" (1912–1913a, p. 141) drives away or kills "his sons, being dangerous to him as rivals" (1925d, p. 68), and the sons unite to kill their father. In the Oedipus myths, Laius fears his son as a rival, abandons him to perish and is ultimately killed by him.

This suggests that Freud's phylogenetic version of the oedipal drama may be a substitutive formation. This suggestion is substantiated not only on the grounds of Freud's contradictory qualifications of this version, but particularly on grounds of the structural identity between this version of the oedipal drama and its mythological presentation.

Substitutive formations and the substituted unconscious are always connected by a common element, the *"tertium comparationis"* (e.g., Freud, 1916–1917a, p. 152). It is this structural identity that permits us to presume that Freud's (1985a, p. 20) "scientific fantasy" is possibly a substitutive formation warding off ideas about the parental influence on their child's inner life which seem to acquire consciousness in a phylogenetic packaging. This presumption corroborates with that of Anzieu (1986), Krüll (1979), and Paul (1996) who are convinced that Freud's father Jacob reappears in the guise of the primal father.

Freud's rejection of the seduction theory and his exclusion of the parental neuroses from the development of the Oedipus complex may well support the impression Jones gained, not however referring to Freud:

> When an analyst loses insight he had previously had, the recurring wave of resistance that has caused the loss is apt to display itself in the form of pseudo-scientific explanations of the data before him, and this is then dignified with the name of a "new theory". Since the source of this is on an unconscious level, it follows that controversy on a purely conscious scientific level is fore-doomed to failure. (Jones, 1955, p. 143)

If one reverses the parent-child situation and thus the perpetrator-victim-relationship implicit in Freud's comment (1896c, pp.207f.) that "the foundation for a neurosis would ... always be laid in childhood by adults" made while still in adherence to his seduction theory, one might suspect that Freud's assumption that oedipal fantasies arising from archaic heritage "invariably seize[s] upon the theme of the parents" (1985c, p. 260) is also a substitutive idea representing the disguised unconscious oedipal fantasies of the parents which invariably seize upon the theme of their child thus displacing the fantasies from the parents onto the child.

Anna Freud's aforementioned fear that there would have been no Oedipus complex, no unconscious fantasies and therefore no psychoanalysis if her father had kept to his seduction theory could only be legitimated if not only the parent's overt seduction of their children were relinquished, but also if their latent seduction tendencies.

Moreover, the myths reveal Freud's phylogenetic justification of the Oedipus complex to be a natural misunderstanding of a pseudo-natural relationship. Fate, phylogentically determined, reveals itself to be a mystified expression of the parental neuroses. Anything that is warded off escapes consciousness, is subjected to the "compulsion to repeat" and—as Dahmer (1973, pp. 379f.) in particular emphasises—achieves its ends just like a natural force, so that the parents' unresolved oedipal problems enforce themselves, as if "blind fate" were at work, in culturally approved forms of child's care and have the same effect as if caused by an archaic heritage.

Even if one is not in agreement with our individual and social-psychological explanation for Freud's resorting to phylogenetic theories, in the face of the material fallacy and considering the onto-genetic origin of the oedipal drama, it seems desirable to follow the myths and Devereux (1953). He argues that there is nothing suggest-ing the presence of pre-existing oedipal wishes in the child and that the Oedipus complex generally "appears to be a consequence of the child's sensitiveness to its parents' [unconscious] sexual and aggressive impulses" (ibid., p. 139; see also Atkins, 1970; Béjarano, 1974; Bernstein, 2001; Laplanche, 1986; Lichtenstein, 1961).

It indeed seems advisable to subscribe to Laplanche's (1986) idea of a generalised seduction and to consider both Freud's early seduction theory and the seduction via unresolved parental oedipal conflicts to be specific cases of a general seduction theory. In the first case, seduc-tion is caused by a pathological conscious and intentional behaviour of adults. In the second case, seduction occurs via unconscious sexual messages, unrecognisable by the parents and addressed to the child in culturally licensed forms of childcare. The cited statements that Freud uses to describe the activities of the parents in the oedipal situa-tion are not only good examples of the unconscious intentions hidden behind the manifest behaviour of the parents, they also suggest that the manifest behaviour of the parents conceals that part of his seduction theory—its latent content—with which he limited its general validity. Among other remarks Freud points out that "affection" for the child "bears the clearest characteristics of a sexual activity, even though of one that is inhibited in its aims" (1910a, p. 47), he talks about the child "as a substitute for a complete sexual object" (1905d, p. 223), as "an erotic plaything" (1912d, p. 181), he terms the mother the child's "first seducer" (1940a, p. 65) who handles the child "with feelings that are derived from her own sexual life" (1905d, p. 223) and who transfers her frustrated "need for love" (1908d, p. 202) onto the child. From this point of view, Freud's descriptions of parental behaviour anticipate Fenichel's answer to Freud's question on 25 February 1914 at a meeting of the Vienna Psychoanalytic Society (Nunberg & Federn, 1975, p. 234) about "the extent to which the Oedipus complex is a reflection of the sexual behaviour of the parents"—namely that the "children's Oedipus complex reflects the parents unsolved Oedipus complex" (Fenichel, 1945, p. 93).

Furthermore, the differing Oedipus myths all have in common that Oedipus can only feel guilty as long as he acts blindly. His self-blinding in Sophocles' *Oedipus Tyrannus* thus opens up a perspective touched on by Graves (1955) allowing a different interpretation than the usual psychoanalytic ones.[1]

In Greek mythology, blindness is associated with sexual guilt (Lampl & Oliver, 1985). The myths dealing with Teiresias' blindness give particular evidence of this. In one myth he is blinded because he has betrayed the sexual secrets of the Gods to humans. In another myth Teiresias is blinded as a punishment for seeing Athena (or Artemis) naked while bathing (Roscher, 1909–1915, p. 183). There is another myth in which Teiresias sees two snakes coupling, violates or slays the female snake and is then transformed into a woman for seven years. Later, seeing them copulating again, he hits or kills the male snake and is transformed back into a man. This transformation was the reason why he was appointed to resolve a dispute between Zeus and Hera. Zeus and Hera were arguing about which sex takes more pleasure in sexual intercourse. They decided to consult Teiresias since he alone had known both experiences. Without hesitation he replied: "οἵην μεν μοῖραν ἀέχα μοιρῶν τέρπεται ἀνήρ, τας ἀέκα ἕ' ἐμπίμπλησι γυνή τέρπουβα νόημα". Teiresias ruled in favour of Zeus who held that the pleasure received by a woman was ten times greater than that of a man. This opinion infuriated Hera, whose view was exactly opposite to her husband's, and she blinded Teiresias, upon which Zeus mitigated his blindness by bestowing on Teiresias the gift of prophecy and longevity extending over the life span of nine generations (Roscher, 1909–1915, pp. 181–187).

Oedipus' self-blinding has sporadically been seen as a destruction of the Sphinx in himself (Balter, 1969), respectively as punishment for his recognition, as resistance against it and as the loss of his recognition (Blum, 1981), furthermore as punishment for the intended matricide (e.g., Faber, 1970), as an extreme form of the desire not to see his own murderous intentions (Goldberger, 1957), as a symbolic sexual act (Kanzer, 1950), as an anticipation of the darkness of his own death (Lederer, 1964), as an attempt to destroy the recognition of his own actions (Rusbridger, 2004), and as a result of not succeeding to prove the crimes of which he accused the blind Teiresias (Stewart, 1961). Stewart justifies this punishment by the talion principle which says that if a person accuses another of committing a specific crime and then fails to prove his case, the accuser will receive a punishment identical with the punishment the accused would have suffered, had he been proved guilty.

In the most cases however, Oedipus' self-blinding is understood as a symbolic castration (Adams, 1988; Abraham, 1913; Bunker, 1944;

Dervin, 1998; Devereux, 1953; Edmunds, 1985; Ferenczi, 1912, p. 15; Fernando, 1998; Freud, 1940a, p. 190; Hartocollis, 2005; Krausz, 1994; Rado, 1956; Shengold, 1963; Thass-Thienemann, 1957; H. A. Van der Sterren, 1952). Graves (1955, p. 376) objects, arguing that Oedipus' self-blinding should not be interpreted as a symbolic castration because castration is described quite openly in other myths. Likewise one could ask why all these factors—the destruction of the Sphinx, the punishment for Oedipus' recognition or intended patricide, the desire not to see his own evil intentions, the sexual act, the darkness of death, destroying the recognition of one's own actions, or the failure to prove to the blind Teiresias the crime of which Oedipus accused him—are in need of symbolic representation.

Neither can Oedipus' self-blinding be understood as a symbolic expression of his unwillingness to see his guilt, as Albarella and Donadio (1989) and Rollo May (1960, p. 38) presume. According to Graves (1955, p. 376), Oedipus' self-blinding is simply a theatrical tool that Sophocles employed to demonstrate that Oedipus saw something that he should not have seen, that is, the guilt of Laius and Jocasta.

One could also argue that Oedipus was not allowed to "see" the knowledge that was hidden in his damaged feet. In Greek "Oidipous" the prefix "oid" is both the root of "oideo" = "swell" as well as "oida" = "know" so that "Oedipus" means both "swollen foot" and "the one who knows about the feet" (see, e.g., Barrat & Straus, 1994; Dunbar-Soule Dobson, 2007; Edmunds, 1988; Rudnytsky, 1987; Steiner, 1994; Thass-Thienemann, 1957). As Miller points out (2006, p. 231), the "oida" in Oedipus identifies him as "knower-of-feet",[2] and Oedipus, like Teiresias, who acquired his knowledge from the birds, acquired his knowledge from the iron with which his ankles were perforated. If so, the entire knowledge in the oedipal drama that Oedipus was blind to, is contained in his swollen feet.

We find support for this when considering that not only Chrysippus, but Teiresias too can be understood as Oedipus' alter ego (e.g., Miller, 2006; Róheim, 1946) and that Teiresias was blinded because he had seen something sexual which he should not have seen. Graves (1955, p. 376) mentions myths in which looking at coupling snakes is dangerous because the witness will be punished with the "'female disease'". Caldwell (1974) understands the disclosure of the secrets of the gods, particularly the copulation of Zeus and Alcmene which Teiresias reveals to Amphitryon, Alcmene's husband, to be a mythological equivalent of the child's desire to observe parental sexuality. According to Róheim (1946; 1953) Teiresias saw the coitus of his parents—"*Father Zeus and Mother Hera having intercourse as serpents*" (1946, p. 316; italics in the original)—, acted out his negative Oedipus complex when observing two coupling snakes and injuring or killing the female snake, then he acted out his positive Oedipus complex by injuring or killing the male snake.

We see support for this in the first production of Sophocles' play in which the actors wore masks and Oedipus's blindness was presented to the Athenian audience by a mask with blood dripping from its eyes (Mann, 1993). Support comes also from a partially preserved drama by Euripides in which Oedipus is blinded as a child or teenager by Laius' soldiers or servants (Gruppe, 1906a, p. 525; Nauck, 1889, Fragment 541), and from another myth (reported by Edmunds, 1985, Gruppe, 1906a, p. 525, and Schneiderhan, 1852, p. 11) in which Oedipus' blinding is caused by his foster father, Polybus.

In the light of all these myths, Sophocles' Oe*dipus Tyrannus* is, as Pilikian (1974, cited in Steiner, 1985, p. 161) indicates in our introductory quotation to this chapter, not a story "about the revelation of truth but about the cover up of truth". It is a cover story that conceals the children's innocence of their own oedipal issues. The story's popularity is not founded on what it presents but on what these presentations transport into the visual field of a blind spot. All responsibility for the Oedipus complex is ascribed to the child. Contrary to Freud's view, the members of the audience did not identify with Oedipus. Rather, as Devereux indicated, one must assume

> that many members of the Greek audience found the play of absorbing interest precisely because they successfully—though perhaps unconsciously—identified themselves with the problems of certain major characters ... the women in Sophocles' audience must have had at least an unconscious empathy with Jocasta's problems ... the male audience must likewise have felt a certain carefully repressed kinship with Laius. (Devereux, 1953, p. 133)

As Breger (2000, p. 137) supposes, it seems as if Sophocles' *Oedipus Tyrannus* constituted a cover story to which Freud adhered because it helped him to hide something from himself. What the subject matter was that Freud wanted to cover up is unknown. While Balmary (1982) and Krüll (1979) believe that it enclosed aspects of his father that Freud did not want to recognise, Breger (2000, p. 137) assumes that in the course of his self-analysis Freud became threatened by overwhelming losses he had experienced in his early years and could not acknowledge in later life.

CHAPTER TWELVE

Oedipus at Colonus—the lost blindness

> And what to us seems merest accident springs from the deepest
> source of destiny.
>
> —Friedrich Schiller, 1789, Act II, Scene 3

Coming to an end, we want to let Sophocles have his speak once more, namely in *Oedipus at Colonus*. This tragedy, as Miller (2006) and Seidenberg and Papathomopoulos (1960) have pointed out, has received far less attention from psychoanalysts than *Oedipus Tyrannus*. Freud's works never mentions the drama. However, in 1906 Freud (1906f, p. 245) subsumes "the tragedies of Sophocles" under the "ten most magnificent works (of world literature)", and in Constans (1881, p. 18) *Oedipus at Colonus* is mentioned at a position shortly before Freud started underlining and also on the pages to follow (ibid., p. 23, p. 40, p. 42, p. 376, p. 382, p. 387). Naiman (1992) also suspects that Freud was familiar with this tragedy, for in later life he liked to call his daughter Anna "my faithful Antigone-Anna" (letter to Ferenczi, 12 October 1928, 1960a, p. 382) or "my faithful Anna-Antigone" (letter to Arnold Zweig, 2 Mai 1935, 1960a, p. 424). Gay (1988) informs us that for Freud, Anna was the most important of his children—like Antigone was for Oedipus—and that Anna was increasingly tied to her father, personally and professionally;

79

and these ties persisted throughout the remainder of their lives. In his later years Freud referred to Anna as Antigone. While Anna became a pioneering child analyst in her own right, she also served as her father's secretary, confidante, representative, colleague, and nurse.

Oedipus at Colonus is regarded as the last of Sophocles' plays, written when he was eighty-nine years old and about twenty-five years after he wrote *Oedipus Tyrannus* (Kanzer, 1948). Kanzer (1948), Lorenz (1916), Michels (1986), Pollock (1986), Rank (1926, p. 145) and Seidenberg and Papathomopoulos (1960) refer to Sophocles' life circumstances. Early in life he married Theoris, a woman of Sicilian birth by whom he had a son, Ariston. Because Theoris was a foreigner, the marriage was not considered legal, nor was the son recognised as his heir. Some years later, Sophocles married Nicostrate, a free Athenian, who bore him four sons, the eldest, Iophon, becoming the legal heir. According to legend, Ariston had a son whom he named Sophocles. This grandson was the darling of the old man's heart. Iophon, also a dramatist, feared that Ariston and his offspring might endear themselves to his father and become his heirs. At a hearing before court Sophocles defended himself solely by reading portions of the *Oedipus at Colonus* which he was currently writing and was acquitted without further dispute. Sophocles forgave his son and a reconciliation ensued.

The drama itself was produced for the first time by his grandson (also called Sophocles) in 401BC. Years after being exiled, the blind and aged Oedipus, led by Antigone, reaches the sacred ground of the Eumenides, hoping to be finally released from his grievous life. Ismene joins the two, willing to help render the gods merciful. Theseus, King of Athens, pities Oedipus and offers him his hospitality.

Creon appears and offers Oedipus a conciliatory return to Thebes because Oedipus' sons, Eteocles and Polynices, are fighting each other for the reign of Thebes and an oracle has prophesised that the city of Thebes only has any future if Oedipus is buried there. Oedipus refuses to return home. Thereafter Creon kidnaps Antigone and Ismene who are then again freed by Theseus.

Later, Oedipus' son Polynices enters, telling his father that he has been unjustly driven out of Thebes by his brother and that he is preparing to attack the city. He wants to help Oedipus get back the throne of Thebes, whose legacy he would then have. Oedipus curses Polyneices because he has never cared about his father. He stresses that he was only able to survive thanks to the care of his daughters, and foretells that his two sons will kill each other in the coming battle over Thebes. Polynices recognises the seriousness of the curse and begs Antigone to bury him should he die in battle. Lightening and thunder occur which, according to the prophesy, announce Oedipus' impending death. Oedipus seeks his burial place on the hill which only Theseus is to know about and has to remain a secret so that Athens remains protected. The gods call for Oedipus and in death he rises to heroic grandeur.

There are very few psychoanalytic interpretations of *Oedipus at Colonus*. Rado (1962) begins his interpretation with the scene in which Oedipus, led by his daughter Antigone, enters the grove of the Eumenides, being unaware of its holy character. This place is foretold by Apollo to be a final refuge for the outcast from Thebes and this prophecy would reveal Oedipus' unconscious state of mind. Rado interprets the entering as a symbol of the forbidden penetration into Jocasta, a penetration of the grove, the "inviolate thicket" (ibid., p. 236) of his mother, with the aim of returning into the maternal womb. Antigone symbolises Jocasta and the whole scenery is condensed in the words: "I did not know what I was doing; Jocasta led me on as does Antigone now" (ibid.).

In Rado's interpretation, Oedipus rejects returning to Thebes and prefers to remain in Athens because his native city has become a symbol of guilt to him—the scene of his parricide and incest—and Athens was "the long sought for virgin mother ... who will take the son into her womb" (ibid., p. 238). Theseus represents the noble and chaste father and Oedipus recreates the infantile fantasy of parents who have no intercourse. The son remains unborn, the mother's virginity is restored and parricide and incest are undone. Rado (1962, pp. 237f.) refers to the choir who express Oedipus' thoughts: "Not to be born beats all philosophy. The second best is to have seen the light, and then go back quickly whence we came".

Oedipus' return into the maternal womb could explain why Oedipus condemns his sons, Polyneices and Eteocles, and prophesises that they will kill each other. They must die, Rado (1962) argues, to undo their shameful birth. Antigone and Ismene, who do not share their brothers' fate, are images of motherly love whom the son loves more than any man (the father) ever will.

Oedipus' insistence on secrecy for his burial place as a condition of Athens' welfare and on Theseus as sole confidant would constitute a reversal of the dreadful fantasy that the father is always present in the mother's womb and that Oedipus is not. In Oedipus' fantasy he now expels the father and has the womb all for himself. At the same time Oedipus splits his father image. His love for the father is redirected to Theseus, his hate to Creon, the evil father. Oedipus' appeal to Theseus to liberate Antigone and Ismene—the mother—before their captors can abduct them, testify to the son's loving submission to the father.

Rado sees Oedipus' end as a reward for his submission. He interprets thunder and lightning as the awesome attributes of Zeus, the deified father, which do not frighten Oedipus, because the god's lightning is "smiling", as the oracle promised, and Zeus' thunder softens to a loving call: "'Oedipus! Oedipus! why are we waiting? You delay too long, too long to come'" (ibid., p. 341). Oedipus follows the call and leaves the world in a manner no-one but Theseus is witness to. The secret of Oedipus' burial is that Oedipus "enters the womb but not to remain there, instead, he joins the father in heaven" (ibid.).

Kanzer (1948) interprets the drama in a similar way. Oedipus undoes his parricide through acknowledging Theseus as his ruler, restores the figure of the father to life, and delegates his powers to the father. Antigone symbolises the mother. By giving up his kingdom and his eyesight, Oedipus renounces gratification of his instincts, and the sacred region symbolises the mother's genitals. He understands the drama as a repetition of the earlier traumatic experiences which terminate differently. Oedipus projects his former self, his guilt, onto Polyneices, Creon who previously banned Oedipus, is now banned himself, instead of parricide there is friendship with the father, represented by Theseus, and Oedipus' death is a kind of wedding ceremony symbolising that the relationship to his mother is now approved of by the gods.

Heiman (1962) too argues that Oedipus projects his guilt onto Polyneices and comes to the conviction that the gods rule the world and that obedience to their authority gives significance to his life and death. Politzer (1972, p. 492) believes that Oedipus projects his guilt onto Thebes.

Steiner (1990) too understands Oedipus' deification at the end of the drama as a disavowal of Oedipus' guilt, a "retreat from truth to omnipotence" (ibid., p. 233). Fromm (1957) interprets the entry into the sacred ground as a reunion with his mother, Seidenberg and Papathomopoulos (1960) and H. A. Van der Sterren (1952) see the death of Oedipus also as a reunion with his mother, whereby the former add that, by virtue of his deification Oedipus disavows his fear of growing older and dying.

Parsons (1990, p. 33) offers another interpretation. Referring to Theseus who says "I am a man too, and I know the difference between us lies only in the fortune of the morrow" and to Theseus' emphasis on the similarity between Oedipus' and Theseus' life histories, she sees Oedipus as a manifestation of the repressed in Theseus.

These interpretations have structures similar to the interpretations of dreams, and as there can be no decision about the accuracy of such interpretations without having worked through the respective life history psychoanalytically, one could leave all these coexisting interpretations uncommented.

We did not mention this second drama because of its action or on account of the structural similarity between the relationship of Oedipus and Antigone and Freud and his daughter Anna, nor did we mention the interpretations, because we regard these as being essentially equivalent.

For example, in Rado's interpretation one might question the grounds leading him to believe that "Oedipus' innermost desire and the prophecy are one, for the oracle speaks always for the hero whose unconscious mind it reveals" (Rado, 1962, p. 236). As aforementioned, Robert (1915, pp. 68f.) noted that the oracle of Delphi was not introduced until later in the Oedipus epic, possibly with the intention of hiding the activities of the parents in the concept of fate, the will of the gods. In this context, one could also assume that the oracle in *Oedipus at Colonus* is indeed a substitutive formation, but not for the unconscious wishes of Oedipus, but of the intentions of Jocasta.

The mystery of how Antigone and Ismene can still be alive and symbolise the good mother when at the same time the undoing of the incest demands their death, remains unsolved. Furthermore, Rado's, Kanzer's (1948) and Parsons' (1990) interpretations fail to justify exactly why Theseus is suitable to represent the chaste and good father. In Greek mythology, Theseus is anything other than good and chaste. Ariadne chooses Theseus as her lover, Theseus not only has a love affair with the wife of Lykomedes, but also with Antiope, Hippolyte, Phaedra (Roscher, 1909–1915, pp. 715–721), Anaxo, Helena, Persephone, Aigle, and Alope (Gruppe, 1906a, pp. 582–589). He appears in one myth as "an originally hostile demon" (ibid., p. 583; translated for this edition) and places a curse on his son Hippolyte because Hippolyte slept with his wife Phaedra (Gruppe, 1906b. p. 877). On his way to Athens he kills several men and is the cause of his father's suicide. For after having killed the Minotaur, Ariadne's father, with her help, he forgets on his home journey to hoist a white flag, which was supposed to signalise the victory to his father Aegeus. He shows a black flag as a sign of his death and his father, seeing the black-sailed ship, kills himself by leaping from a cliff into the sea.[1]

The main reason for including this drama and its interpretations is that in it Sophocles presents those matters hidden to Oedipus in *Oedipus Tyrannus*, those matters which were hidden to Freud and are also misunderstood in the cited interpretations.

Although differing in their details, the above-mentioned interpretations have in common that they interpret Sophocles' *Oedipus at Colonus* in the light of the Oedipus complex. In their interpretations the drama is either understood as a hidden presentation of the Oedipus complex (H. A. Van der Sterren, 1952) or as a staging of Oedipus' defence, warding off his guilt to the crimes he had committed in *Oedipus Tyrannus*. Rado (1962) regards those actions that made Oedipus responsible for his guilt as being undone, in Parsons' (1990) view Oedipus' actions are transferred to Theseus and are warded off by him, Heiman (1962) and Kanzer (1948) see the guilt projected onto Polynices, Politzer (1972) onto Thebes, and Steiner (1990) sees the guilt disavowed by way of omnipotence and deification.

However, these interpretations inform us only seemingly about the latent content in the manifest text. In reality they mystify the manifest content of the drama and present it in a distorted manner. Certainly, the manifest story of *Oedipus at Colonus* reveals, as Hadas (1950, pp. 84f.) rightly notes, "Oedipus' disclaimer of guilt ... when he had acknowledged guilt in the earlier *Oedipus*". Yet the guilt for the crimes that Oedipus ascribes to himself at the end of *Oedipus Tyrannus* is not warded off in *Oedipus at Colonus*. In this drama, Oedipus does not retreat from the truth, as Kanzer (1948) supposes, but comes closer to the truth. He realises that he has taken the guilt for actions, for which in reality Jocasta and Laius were responsible.

If the interpreting authors had not focused on *Oedipus at Colonus* through the lens of the Freudian Oedipus complex but turned their attention to the Oedipus myths, they might have noticed that in this play Oedipus regains his sight and sees the issues revealed by the Oedipus myths that Freud could only understand in a phylogenetically mystified manner.

Following on Oedipus' self-blinding at the end of *Oedipus Tyrannus* a servant reports that Oedipus said that his eyes "will never see the crime I have committed or had done upon me" (Sophocles, 1991a, 1271–1272). Oedipus now announces: "In all that I speak there will be vision" (Sophocles, 1889, 74), declares that he is not to be regarded "as a lawless man" (ibid., 141), and the chorus promises, "No man is visited by the punishment of fate if he requites deeds which were first done to himself" (ibid., 229–239). Oedipus continues:

> my acts, at least, have been in
> suffering rather than doing—if I must mention the tale of
> my mother and my father, because of which you fear me.
> That know I full well. And yet how was I innately evil?
> I, who was merely requiting a wrong, so that, had I been
> acting with knowledge, even then I could not be accounted
> evil. But, as it was, all unknowing I went where I went
> —while they who wronged me knowingly sought my ruin
> (ibid., 266–274).

In conflict with Creon, Oedipus emphasises that he inadvertently endured murder and incest, killed his father without knowing his identity and had children with Jocasta "to *her* shame" (ibid., 984; our italics). Furthermore, Oedipus claims that if in danger of being killed, Creon would surely not ask whether the offender might be his father, he would react and fight back immediately.

The choir shares Oedipus' view: "Many were the sorrows that came to him without cause, but a just divinity will lift him up again" (ibid., 1568f.). Oedipus deification does not take place in the course of defence, as Kanzer (1948) assumes, but as compensation for the unjustified harm that befell him.

We mentioned earlier that in Greek mythology blindness is associated with sexual guilt (Lampl & Oliver, 1985). So it is not surprising that Oedipus, when recognising his innocence (Bilmes, 1999; J. Jones, 1976; Rudnystky, 1999), loses the blindness that he inflicted on himself in *Oedipus Tyrannus* with Jocasta's clasp. He realises that he has taken the blame for actions for which Laius and Jocasta were responsible. At the end of *Oedipus at Colonus*, Oedipus tells Theseus:

> Immediately, with no hand to guide me,
> I will lead to the place where I must. (Sophocles, 1889,
> 1520–1521)

Addressing his daughters, Antigone and Ismene, he continues:

> Children, follow me. For now in turn it is I
> that shine forth wondrously as a leader for you,
> as you were your father's. Onward.
> Do not touch me, but allow me unaided to find
> the sacred tomb where it is my fate to be buried in this land
> (ibid., 1543–1547).

The regained vision allows him to detect that which was hidden from him in *Oedipus Tyrannus*, namely that he did not commit patricide and incest with his mother as a perpetrator, but as a victim.

As soon as Oedipus becomes aware that his fate has been forced upon him by his parents, he realises that he has lived in a false life: He has no Oedipus complex.

In *Oedipus at Colonus* this knowledge is still mystified. With the call of God Zeus: "Oh, you, yes, you know where you stay, Oedipus? What should the seams? For too long we are waiting for you" (ibid., 1627–1628) the drama comes to an end with a reconciliation with the father in death and Oedipus' deification, not only suggesting that when bearing the blame of others one can ascend to the Gods but also that the oedipal drama is resolved by its recognition. However, the myths teach us that this is not the case. Oedipus' recognition does not prevent the oedipal drama Laius and Jocasta were engaged in and transferred to him being passed on to his offspring.

We would like to substantiate this somewhat. Ismene and Antigone are dishonoured, raped or killed in the temple of Hera by Laodamos (Roscher, 1890–1897, p. 550; Gruppe, 1906a, p. 533), the son of Eteocles. Polynices and Eteocles, sons of Oedipus, were deadly accursed by Oedipus because they did not object to his banishment from Thebes, no longer honoured him as King (ibid., p. 526; Preller, 1875, p. 344; Roscher, 1897–1909, p. 2663) and gave more importance to the throne than to the father.

In the aforementioned myth in which the Gods discover the incest of Jocasta and Oedipus immediately and Jocasta hangs herself whereas Oedipus remains King of Thebes, Jocasta, in the guise of the Erinyes, allies with their sons to punish Oedipus most effectively by ingratitude (Roscher, 1897–1909, p. 701). In this case the curse that Oedipus imposed upon his sons is a reaction to their ingratitude. But some myths also know of an oracle which causes the exposure of both sons, at least of Polynices (Gruppe, 1906a, p. 525; Roscher, 1897–1909, p. 2662). The sons kill each other in their struggle for the throne of Thebes, and Antigone, being engaged to Creon's son Haemon, decides not to follow Creon's order not to bury her brother Polynices. She buries him, is caught, and buried alive.

Oedipus' exposure is reproduced in the deadly curse on or exposure of Eteocles and Polynices, the relationship between Jocasta and Oedipus, directed against Laius, is reproduced in the connection between Jocasta and her sons Eteocles and Polynices, which was directed against Oedipus, and Jocasta's and Oedipus' incest crops up in a mystified form in the relationships between Ismene, Antigone, and Laodamos (aunts and nephew), Antigone and Haemon (cousins), and Antigone and Polynices (brother and sister).

The passionate love Antigone has for Polynices in Sophocles' (1991b) drama *Antigone* has been emphasised by several authors. Bowra (1944, p. 95) talks of an "intense love for her brother", Seidenberg and Papathomopoulos (1962, p. 103) understand Antigone's behaviour as "the tragic outcome of incestuous wishes", and Werman (1979, p. 459) is convinced that the assumption "of her incestuous yearnings for Polyneices cannot be faulted". In these judgements these authors are referring to statements Antigone makes such as:

> I myself will bury him. It will be good
> To die, so doing. I shall lie by his side
> Loving him as he loved me (Sophocles, 1991b, 72–74)
> Tomb, bridal chamber, prison forever (ibid., 892)
> But when I come
> to that other world my hope is strong
> that my coming will be welcome to my father,
> and dear to you, my mother, and dear to you
> my brother, deeply loved …
> Had I been a mother

of children and my husband been dead and rotten
I would not have taken this weary task upon me
against the will of the city …
If my husband were dead I might have has another,
And child from another man, if I lost the first.
But when father and mother both were hidden in death
no brother's life would bloom for me again.
That is the law under which I gave you precedence,
My dearest brother, and this is why Creon thinks me wrong.
(ibid., 896–915)

With reference to Sadger's (1910, pp. 60f.) remark that "the wish to die together is the wish to sleep and lie together" and to wake up again in an inner transfigured state of eternal union and internal happiness, Almansi (1991) argues convincingly that underlying the manifest behaviour of Antigone in Sophocles' drama we detect her incestuous wishes, originally directed towards her father Oedipus and later displaced onto Polynices and Haemon. These would be the reason why Antigone hangs herself like her mother Jocasta did, and Haemon, when seeing his hanged fiancé, stabs himself to death in a manner similar to which Oedipus stabs his eyes when he saw the hanged Jocasta.

Finally, we want to reiterate our central argument: it is not the Oedipus complex that informs us about the latent content of the Oedipus myths, but the Oedipus myths that inform us about the latent content of Freud's Oedipus complex. If we add the Oedipus myths to the Oedipus complex, there can be no doubt about Bowras' (1944, p. 349) observation: "At the end of *Oedipus at Colonus* no unresolved discords remain, no mysteries call for an answer." Summarising briefly with reference to the statement by Horkheimer and Adorno (1944, p. XVIII) quoted at the beginning, myths enlighten the Oedipus complex and revert Freud's enlightenment into a myth. They demystify this complex, revealing it to be a drama in which the rivalry of the mother with her daughter stems from the mother's oedipal problems and is initiated by the father's preference for his daughter, and in which the father's rivalry with his son is caused by his oedipal problems and instigated by the mother's preference for her son.

NOTES

Chapter One

1. In the myths Oedipus' injury is represented differently. In Sophocles (1991a, line 718) Laius "pierced his ankles", in Graves (1955, p. 371) and Preller (1921, p. 884) Oedipus' feet are pierced, in Robert (1915, p. 72) the heels, in Rank (1926, p. 210) and Roscher (1897–1909, p. 705) the ankles are pierced with a nail. As in the English speaking eras the injury is predominantly described as "pierced ankles", we decided to use this term.

2. There is a version of the Judas legend showing the greatest similarity to the Oedipus' fable. In this, Judas' mother brands a sign on his back with a hot iron before abandoning him. This enables her to recognise him after the incestuous marriage (Rank, 1926, p. 278).

3. Freud (1925i, p. 132) only mentions this issue.

4. In English: "There was once that came to Laius and told him that he should die a victim of the hands his son, a son to be born of Laius and me" (Sophocles, 1991, 711–714).

5. In Armstrong's (2007) view, Freud used Constans' (1881) book to inform himself after writing to Fliess: "Comments on Oedipus Rex, the talisman fairy tale, and possibly Hamlet, will find their place. I first must

read up on the Oedipus legend—do not yet know where" (letter to Fliess, 15 March 1898, Freud, 1985c, p. 304).

Chapter Two

1. In two other papers of the same year, Freud (1896a, p. 152; 1896b, p. 163) refers to "thirteen patients" he had treated. If one assumes that he had exaggerated the degree of treatment success, treating thirteen out of eighteen patients successfully would still be a very satisfactory cure rate.

Chapter Three

1. Jones (1953, p. 319) reports that Freud started with his self-analysis in summer 1897 and ended it according to Anzieu (1986) in 1901.
2. Freud (1900a, p. 256) states that it is "as though boys regarded their fathers and girls their mothers as their rivals in love, whose elimination could not fail to be to their advantage." This equality between boys and girls in their oedipal rivalry is not maintained consistently. For instance, in 1931 Freud rejected the term "Electra complex" to designate the female Oedipus complex as proposed by Jung, arguing that this term "seeks to emphasize the analogy between the attitude of the two sexes" whereas in his view it "is only in the male child that we find the fateful combination of love for the one parent and simultaneous hatred for the other as a rival" (Freud, 1931b, p. 229). But at the end of his life he seems implicitly to ascribe an oedipal rivalry to females: "It does little harm to a woman if she remains in her feminine Oedipus attitude. (The term 'Electra complex' has been proposed for it)" (1940a, p. 194). However, the Oedipus and the Electra myths do not have the same structure (see, e.g., Dervin, 1998). Agamemnon, father of Electra and Orestes, kills Tantalus, the first husband of Clytemnestra and their child and forces Clytemnestra to marry him. Furthermore, he approves the sacrifice of Iphigenia on Aulis, and coming back from the Trojan war he brings Cassandra, Priamos' daughter, as his mistress with him. Agamemnon and Cassandra are killed by Aegisthus, the lover of Clytemnestra and/or by Clytemnestra, the mother of Electra and Orestes. Prompted by the oracle of Delphi to avenge the death of his father, Orestes returns a few years later, and, together with Electra, kills his mother and Aegisthus (Graves, 1955, p. 413ff.; Roscher, 1884–1890, pp. 1236ff.).

Chapter Four

1. With reference to Freud's (1931b, p. 226) statement "we must retract the universality of the thesis that the Oedipus complex is the nucleus of the neuroses" Hartocollis (2005) believes that Freud abandoned his thesis of the universality of the Oedipus complex. Yet after this statement Freud continues: "But if anyone feels reluctant about making this correction, there is no need for him to do so".

Chapter Six

1. According to one mythological version, Oedipus does not beget his four children with Jocasta but with Eurygonia, his second wife. Christ (1905, p. 223) and Robert (1915, p. 111), however, indicated that Eurygonia is not the name of another person but another name for Jocasta. Astymedusa and Epicaste are other names by which Jocasta appears in Greek mythology (ibid., p. 180).
2. English: "They said that he should kill his parents" (Sophocles, 1991, 1176).
3. Even as early as 1912 Rank (1926, p. 210) talks about "the father's fear of retribution".
4. In analysing one of his dreams, Freud also discovers "the envy which is felt for the young by those who have grown old, but which they believe they have completely stifled" (1900a, p. 560). Yet he doesn't give it a systematic significance.
5. The different meanings attributed to the sphinx are summarised in Reik (1920).
6. On the contrary, Freud (1928b, p. 188) regards the Sphinx as "the monster who symbolises the father".
7. Moreover, the death of the Sphinx following the revelation of Jocasta's secrets also confirms the assumption that the Sphinx was introduced into the drama to conceal Jocasta's secrets. With the revelation of these secrets, the existence of the Sphinx becomes superfluous.
8. In addition to our arguments in favour of regarding Jocasta and the Sphinx as one person, we want to mention that in Greek mythology the Sphinx is also the offspring of an incest. In one myth, the Sphinx is the daughter of Echidna, half woman, the other half a gigantic agile serpent (Roscher, 1884–1890, p. 1212), and her son Orthus is a being with two dog's heads and seven dragon's heads, fathered by Typhaon (1897–1909, p. 1215).

Chapter Seven

1. Further arguments against Masson's idea can be found in Kupfersmid (1992).

Chapter Eight

1. To our knowledge, this statement has not been discussed or quoted extensively in the analytic literature. It is only mentioned by four authors (Fuchsman, 2001; Hartocollis, 2005; Lax, 1995, 2007; Sapisochin, 1999).
2. Melanie Klein comes rather close to this notion: "The unconscious theory that her mother contains the admired and desired penis of the father underlies, in my experience, many of the phenomena which Freud described as the relation of the girl to the phallic mother" (Klein, 1945, p. 32).

Chapter Eleven

1. Further, non-psychoanalytic interpretations of Oedipus' self-blinding are summarised in Caldwell (1974).
2. In Constans' (1881) book Freud underlined the passage containing the etymology of Oedipus' name, "'the one who knows the enigma of the foot'" (Steiner, 1994, p. 522).

Chapter Twelve

1. Gide (1950, p. 49) notes that Theseus "purposely forget[s]" to hoist the white sail in order to get rid of his father and to become King of Athens.

REFERENCES

Abraham, K. (1909). Traum und Mythus. Eine Studie zur Völkerpsychologie. In: K. Abraham *Psychoanalytische Studien I* (pp. 261–323). Frankfurt/M: Fischer, 1971.

Abraham, K. (1913). Restrictions and transformations of scopophilia in psycho-neurotics; with remarks on analogous phenomena in folk-psychology. In: K. Abraham *Selected papers* (pp. 169–234). London: Maresfield, 1988.

Abraham, K. (1920). Manifestations of the female castration complex. *The International Journal of Psychoanalysis, 3*: 1–29, 1922.

Adams, L. (1988). Apollo and Marsyas: A metaphor of creative conflict. *The Psychoanalytic Review, 75*: 319–338.

Albarella, C., & Donadio, M. (1989). Oedipus and the delusion of reason. *Rivista Italiana di Psicoanalysi, 35*: 106–136.

Allen, A. (1965). Stealing as a defense. *The Psychoanalytic Quarterly, 34*: 572–583.

Almansi, R. J. (1991). A psychoanalytic study of Sophocles' Antigone. *The Psychoanalytic Quarterly, 60*: 69–85.

Anzieu, D. (1986). *Freud's Self-Analysis*. New York, NY: International Psychoanalytic Library.

Armstrong, R. H. (2007). The archaeology of Freud's reading. *Psychoanalysis and History, 9*: 251–259.

Atkins, N. B. (1970). The Oedipus myth, adolescence, and the succession of generations. *Journal of the American Psychoanalytic Association, 18*: 860–875.

Bak, R. C. (1953). Fetishism. *Journal of the American Psychoanalytic Association, 1*: 285–298.

Balmary, M. (1982). *Psychoanalyzing Psychoanalysis. Freud and the Hidden Fault of the Father.* Baltimore: John Hopkins University Press.

Balter, L. (1969). The mother as source of power a psychoanalytic study of three Greek myths. *The Psychoanalytic Quarterly, 38*: 217–274.

Barrat, B. B., & Straus, B. R. (1994). Toward postmodern masculinities. *American Imago, 51*: 37–67.

Basch, M. F. (1986). How does analysis cure? An appreciation. *Psychoanalytic Inquiry, 6*: 403–428.

Basch, M. F. (1987). The interpersonal and the intrapsychic: Conflict or harmony. *Contemporary Psychoanalysis, 23*: 367–381.

Béjarano, A. (1974). A discussion of the paper by Claude le Guen on "The formation of the transference". *The International Journal of Psychoanalysis, 55*: 513–518.

Beres, D., & Obers, J. (1950). The effects of extreme deprivation in infancy on psychic structure in adolescence. *The Psychoanalytic Study of the Child, 5*: 212–228.

Bergmann, M. S. (1988). On the fate of the intrapsychic image of the psychoanalyst after termination of the analysis. *The Psychoanalytic Study of the Child, 43*: 137–153.

Bergmann, M. S. (1993). Reflections on the history of psychoanalysis. *Journal of the American Psychoanalytic Association, 41*: 929–955.

Bernstein, A. (2001). Freud and Oedipus: A new look at the Oedipus complex in the light of Freud's life. *Modern Psychoanalysis, 26*: 269–282.

Bick, I. J. (1989). Aliens among us: a representation of children in science fiction. *Journal of the American Psychoanalytic Association, 37*: 737–775.

Bilmes, M. (1999). Psychoanalysis and morals: a dark alliance. *The Psychoanalytic Review, 86*: 627–642.

Bion, W. R. (1963). *Elements of Psycho-Analysis.* London: Heinemann.

Blanck, G. (1984). The complete Oedipus complex. *The International Journal of Psychoanalysis, 65*: 331–339.

Blass, R. B., & Simon, B. (1994). The value of the historical perspective to contemporary psychoanalysis: Freud's "seduction hypothesis". *The International Journal of Psychoanalysis, 75*: 677–694.

Bloch, D. (1989). Freud's retraction of his seduction theory and the Schreber case. *The Psychoanalytic Review, 76*: 185–201.

Blos, P. (1989). The place of the adolescent process in the analysis of the adult. *The Psychoanalytic Study of the Child, 44*: 3–17.

Blum, H. P. (1981). The forbidden quest and the analytic ideal: The superego and insight. *The Psychoanalytic Quarterly, 50*: 535–556.

Bonomi, C. (1996). Mute correspondence. *International Forum of Psychoanalysis, 5*: 165–189.

Bowra, C. M. (1944). *Sophoclean Tragedy*. Oxford: Oxford University Press.

Bradley, R. N. (1926). *Racial Origins of English Character*. London: Allen and Unwin.

Breger, L. (2000). *Freud. Darkness in the Midst of Vision*. New York, NY: Wiley.

Bross, J. M. (1984). Oedipus and Jocasta: A reexamination of Freud's drama of destiny. In: G. M. Pollock & J. M. Ross (Eds.) *The Oedipus Papers* (pp. 317–338). Madison, CT: International Universities Press, 1988.

Brown, W. (1927). General: Charles S. Myers. Freudian psychology: A lecture given at the institute of pathology and research, St. Mary's Hospital, June 3, 1926. Lancet, 19 June 1926. *The International Journal of Psychoanalysis, 8*: 77–79.

Bunker, H. E. (1944). Mother-murder in myth and legend—A psychoanalytic note. *The Psychoanalytic Quarterly, 13*: 198–207.

Burgner, M. (1985). The oedipal experience: Effects on development of an absent father. *The International Journal of Psychoanalysis, 66*: 311–320.

Burstein, A. G., & Gillian, J. (1997). Teaching Freud: A lesson. *Psychoanalytic Psychology, 14*: 457–473.

Caldwell, R. S. (1974). The blindness of Oedipus. *The International Review of Psycho-Analysis, 1*: 207–218.

Ceccarelli, P. R. (2003). May I call you father? *International Forum of Psychoanalysis, 12*: 197–205.

Christ, W. (1905). *Geschichte der griechischen Literatur bis auf die Zeit Justinians*. Munich: Beck.

Clark, P. L. (1923). Unconscious motives underlying the personalities of great statesmen and their relation to epoch-making events: III The narcism of Alexander the Great. *The Psychoanalytic Review, 10*: 56–69.

Constans, L. (1881). *La Légende d'Œdipe: Étudiée dans l'Antiquité, au Moyen Age et dans les Temps Modernes en Particulier dans le Roman de Thèbes, Texte Français du XIIe Siècle*. Paris: Maisonneuve et C. Libraires.

Dahl, E. K. (1996). The concept of penis envy revisited: A child analyst listens to adult women. *The Psychoanalytic Study of the Child, 51*: 303–325.

Dahmer, H. (1973). *Libido und Gesellschaft*. Frankfurt/M: Suhrkamp.

Davies, J. K., & Fichtner, G. (Eds.) (2006). *Freuds Bibliothek. Vollständiger Katalog*. Tübingen: edition discord.

Dervin, D. (1998). The Electra complex: A history of misrepresentations. *Gender & Psychoanalysis 3*: 451–470.

De Saussure, R. (1920). Le complexe de Jocaste. *Internationale Zeitschrift der Psychoanalyse* 6: 118–122.

Devereux, G. (1953). Why Oedipus killed Laius—A note on the complementary Oedipus complex in Greek drama. *The International Journal of Psychoanalysis, 34*: 132–141.

Devereux, G. (1956). *Normal and abnormal.* In: G. Devereux *Basic Problems in Ethnopsychiatry* (pp. 3–71). Chicago, IL: University of Chicago Press, 1980.

Devereux, G. (1960). Retaliatory homosexual triumph over the father—A further contribution to the counter-oedipal sources of the Oedipus complex. *The International Journal of Psychoanalysis, 41*: 157–161.

Dunbar-Soule Dobson, M. W. (2007). Freud, Kohut, Sophocles: Did Oedipus do wrong? *International Journal of Psychoanalytic Self Psychology, 2*: 53–76.

Eastman, J. (2005). Freud, the Oedipus complex, and Greece or the silence of Athena. *The Psychoanalytic Review, 92*: 335–354.

Edmunds, L. (1985). Freud and the father: Oedipus complex and Oedipus myth. *Psychoanalysis and Contemporary Thought, 8*: 87–103.

Edmunds, L. (1988). The body of Oedipus. *The Psychoanalytic Review, 75*: 51–66.

Edmunds, L., & Ingber, R. (1977). Psychoanalytical writings on the Oedipus legend: A bibliography. *American Imago, 34*: 374–386.

Eigen, M. (1975). The differentiation of an androgynous imago. *The Psychoanalytic Review, 62*: 601–613.

Eissler, K. R. (1993). Comments on erroneous interpretations of Freud's seduction theory. *Journal of the American Psychoanalytic Association, 41*: 571–584.

Etchegoyen, A. (1993). Latency—A reappraisal. *The International Journal of Psychoanalysis, 74*: 347–356.

Faber, M. (1970). Self-destruction in Oedipus Rex. *Imago, 27*: 41–51

Fenichel, O. (1930). The pregenital antecedents of the Oedipus complex. *The International Journal of Psychoanalysis, 12*: 141–166, 1931.

Fenichel, O. (1931). Specific forms of the Oedipus complex. *The International Journal of Psychoanalysis, 2*: 412–430.

Fenichel, O. (1945). *The Psychoanalytic Theory of Neurosis.* London: Routledge & Kegan, 1966.

Ferenczi, S. (1912). The symbolic representation of the pleasure and reality principles in the Oedipus myth. In: G. H. Pollock & J. M. Ross (Eds.) *The Oedipus Papers* (pp. 9–20). Madison, CT: International Universities Press, 1988.

Ferenczi, S. (1932). Confusion of the tongues between the adults and the child—(The language of tenderness and of passion). *The International Journal of Psychoanalysis, 30*: 225–230, 1949.

Fernando, J. (1998). Foot symbolism. *Canadian Journal of Psychoanalysis, 6*: 309–320.

Fitzpatrick-Hanly, M. A. (2007). Object loss, renewed mourning, and psychic change in Jane Austen's persuasion. *The International Journal of Psychoanalysis, 88*: 1001–1017.

Frampton, M. F. (1991). Considerations on the role of Brentano's concept of intentionality in Freud's reputation of the seduction theory. *The International Journal of Psychoanalysis, 18*: 27–36.

Freeman, D. (1967). Totem and taboo: A reappraisal. In: W. Münsterberger (Ed.) *Man and his Culture: Psychoanalytic Anthropology after Totem and Taboo* (pp. 53–78). New York, NY: Taplinger.

Freemantle, A. (1950). The oedipal legend in Christian hagiology. *The Psychoanalytic Quarterly, 19*: 408–409.

Freud, S. (1893f).[1] Charcot. *S. E., 3*: 11–23. London: Hogarth.

Freud, S. (1895d). Studies on hysteria. *S. E., 2*. London: Hogarth.

Freud, S. (1896a). Heredity and the aetiology of neurosis. *S. E., 3*: 143–156. London: Hogarth.

Freud, S. (1896b). Further remarks on the neuro-psychoses of defence. *S. E., 3*: 159–184. London: Hogarth.

Freud, S. (1896c). The aetiology of hysteria. *S. E., 3*: 187–221. London: Hogarth.

Freud, S. (1898a). Sexuality in the aetiology of the neuroses. *S. E., 3*: 259–285. London: Hogarth.

Freud, S. (1900a). *The Interpretation of Dreams. S. E., 4/5*. London: Hogarth.

Freud, S. (1901a). On dreams. *S. E., 5*: 633–686. London: Hogarth.

Freud, S. (1901b). *The Psychopathology in Everyday Life. S. E., 6*. London: Hogarth.

Freud, S. (1905d). Three essays on the theory of sexuality. *S. E., 7*: 123–243. London: Hogarth.

Freud, S. (1905e). Fragment of an analysis of a case of hysteria. *S. E., 7*: 1–122. London: Hogarth.

Freud, S. (1906a). My views on the part played by sexuality in the aetiology of the neuroses. *S. E., 7*: 271–279. London: Hogarth.

Freud, S. (1906f). Contribution to a questionnaire on reading. *S. E., 9*: 245–247. London: Hogarth.

Freud, S. (1908c). On the sexual theories of children. *S. E., 9*: 205–226. London: Hogarth.

Freud, S. (1908d). "Civilized" sexual morality and modern nervous illness. *S. E., 9*: 177–204. London: Hogarth.

---

[1] The years in which Freud's papers were published are given according to Meyer-Palmedo, I. & Fichtner, G. (1999). *Freud Bibliographie mit Werkkonkordanz*. Frankfurt/M: Fischer.

Freud, S. (1908e). Creative writers and day-dreaming. S. E., 9: 141–150. London: Hogarth.

Freud, S. (1909b). Analysis of a phobia in a five-year-old boy. S. E., 10: 5–147. London: Hogarth.

Freud, S. (1910a). Five lectures on psycho-analysis. S. E., 11: 1–56. London: Hogarth.

Freud, S. (1910c). Leonardo da Vinci and a memory of his childhood. S. E., 11: 57–137. London: Hogarth.

Freud, S. (1910h). A special type of object choice made by men. S. E., 11: 163–175. London: Hogarth.

Freud, S. (1912c). Types of onset of neurosis. S. E., 12: 227–238. London: Hogarth.

Freud, S. (1912d). On the universal tendency to debasement in the sphere of love (Contributions to the psychology of love II). S. E., 11: 177–190. London: Hogarth.

Freud, S. (1912–1913a). Totem and Taboo. S. E., 13: 7–161. London: Hogarth.

Freud, S. (1913f). The theme of the three caskets. S. E., 12: 289–301. London: Hogarth.

Freud, S. (1914d). On the history of the psychoanalytic movement. S. E., 14: 7–66. London: Hogarth.

Freud, S. (1915b). Thoughts for the times on war and death. S. E., 14: 273–300. London: Hogarth.

Freud, S. (1915d). Repression. S. E., 14: 141–158. London: Hogarth.

Freud, S. (1915h). Preface to the third edition of three essays on the theory of sexuality. S. E., 7: 130–132. London: Hogarth.

Freud, S. (1916–1917a). Introductory Letters to Psycho-Analysis (Parts I and II). S. E., 15. London: Hogarth.

Freud, S. (1917b). A childhood recollection from Dichtung und Wahrheit. S. E., 17: 145–156. London: Hogarth.

Freud, S. (1918b). From the history of an infantile neurosis. S. E., 17: 1–124. London: Hogarth.

Freud, S. (1919e). A child is being beaten. A contribution to the study of the origin of sexual perversions. S. E., 17: 175–204. London: Hogarth.

Freud, S. (1921c). Group psychology the analysis of the ego. S. E., 18: 65–143.

Freud, S. (1923b). The ego and the id. S. E., 19: 1–66. London: Hogarth.

Freud, S. (1924d). The dissolution of the Oedipus complex. S. E., 19: 171–179. London: Hogarth.

Freud, S. (1924f). A short account of psycho-analysis. S. E., 19: 191–209. London: Hogarth.

Freud, S. (1925d). An autobiographical study. S. E., 20: 7–70. London: Hogarth.

Freud, S. (1925i). Some additional notes on dream-interpretation as a whole. S. E., 19: 123–138. London: Hogarth.

Freud, S. (1925j). Some psychical consequences of the anatomical distinction between the sexes. *S. E., 19*: 241–258. London: Hogarth.

Freud, S. (1926d). Inhibitions, symptoms, and anxiety. *S. E., 20*: 87–172. London: Hogarth.

Freud, S. (1926e). The question of lay analysis. *S. E., 20*: 177–258. London: Hogarth.

Freud, S. (1927c). The future of an illusion. *S. E., 21*: 1–56. London: Hogarth.

Freud, S. (1927e). Fetishism. *S. E., 21*: 152–157. London: Hogarth.

Freud, S. (1928b). Dostoevsky and parricide. *S. E., 21*: 173–194. London: Hogarth.

Freud, S. (1930a). Civilization and its discontent. *S. E., 21*: 57–145.

Freud, S. (1931b). Female sexuality. *S. E., 21*: 221–244. London: Hogarth.

Freud, S. (1932a). The acquisition and control of fire. *S. E., 22*: 183–193. London: Hogarth.

Freud, S. (1933a). *New introductory Letters on Psycho-Analysis. S. E., 22*: 1–182. London: Hogarth.

Freud, S. (1937c). Analysis terminable and interminable. *S. E., 23*: 211–253. London: Hogarth.

Freud, S. (1937d). Constructions in analysis. *S. E., 23*: 257–269. London: Hogarth.

Freud, S. (1939a). *Moses and Monotheism. S. E., 23*: 1–137. London: Hogarth.

Freud, S. (1940a). An outline of psycho-analysis, *S. E., 23*: 141–207. London: Hogarth.

Freud, S. (1940e). Splitting of the ego in the process of defence. *S. E., 23*: 275–278.

Freud, S. (1960a). *Letters of Sigmund Freud, 1873–1939*. Freud, E., & Freud, L. (Eds.). New York, NY: Basic Books.

Freud, S. (1963a). *Psychoanalysis and Faith: The Letters of Sigmund Freud and Oskar Pfister*. Meng, H., & Freud, E. L. (Eds.). London: Hogarth.

Freud, S. (1965a). *The complete Correspondence of Sigmund Freud and Karl Abraham 1907–1925*. Falzeder, E., & Brabant, E. (Eds.). London: Karnac, 2002.

Freud, S. (1974a). *The Freud/Jung Letters: The Correspondence between Sigmund Freud and C. G. Jung*. McGuire, W., & Sauerländer, W. (Eds.). New York, NY: Basic Books.

Freud, S. (1985a). Overview of the transference neurosis. In: I. Grubrich-Simitis (Ed.) A phylogenetic fantasy (pp. 5–20). Cambridge: Harvard University Press, 1987.

Freud, S. (1985c). *The complete Letters of Sigmund Freud to Wilhelm Fliess 1887–1904*. Masson, J. M. (Ed.) London: Belknap, 1985.

Freud, S. (1992a). *The Sigmund Freud-Ludwig Binswanger Correspondence 1908–1938*. Fichtner, G. (Ed.). New York, NY: Other Press, 2003.

Freud, S. (1992g). *The Correspondence of Sigmund Freud and Sándor Ferenczi (Volume I), 1908–1914 (Volume III/2), 1925–1933*. Brabant, E. Falzeder, E., & Giampieri-Deutsch, P. (Eds.) Cambridge: Harvard University Press, 1993.

Fromm, E. (1957). Symbol language in myth, fairy tale, ritual, and novel. In: G. M. Pollock & J. M. Ross (Eds.) *The Oedipus Papers* (pp. 117–142). Madison, CT: International Universities Press, 1988.

Fromm, E. (1959). *Sigmund Freud's Mission. An Analysis of his Personality and Influence*. New York, NY: Harper & Brothers, 1972.

Fuchsman, K. (2001). What does Freud mean by the Oedipus Complex? *Free Associations, 9A*: 82–118.

Furman, R. A. (1988). Object removal revisited. *The International Review of Psycho-Analysis, 15*: 165–176.

Galdstone, I. (1976). Sophocles contra Freud: Reassessment of the Oedipus complex. In: I. Galdstone (Ed.) *Psychiatry and the Human Condition* (pp. 248–262). New York, NY: Brunner.

Garcia, E. E. (1987). Freud's seduction theory. *The Psychoanalytic Study of the Child, 42*: 443–468.

Gay, P. (1988). *Freud. A Life for our Time*. New York, NY: Norton.

Gicklhorn, J., & Gicklhorn, R. (1960). *Sigmund Freuds akademische Laufbahn im Lichte der Dokumente*. Wien: Urban und Schwarzenberg.

Gide, A. (1950). *Two legends: Oedipus and Theseus*. New York, NY: Vintage.

Gill, H. S. (1987). Effects of oedipal triumph caused by collapse or death of the rival parent. *The International Journal of Psychoanalysis, 68*: 251–260.

Gitelson, M. (1952). Re-evaluation of the role of the Oedipus complex. *The International Journal of Psychoanalysis, 33*: 351–354.

Goldberger, E. (1957). The id and the ego: A development interpretation: Part IV. *The Psychoanalytic Review, 44*: 280–288.

Graves, R. (1955). *The Greek Myths*. London: Penguin, 2011.

Greenberg, J. (1987). Discussion. *Contemporary Psychoanalysis, 23*: 391–400.

Greenberg, J. (2003). Commentary on "Psychoanalytic discourse at the turn of our century: A plea for a measure of humility". *Journal of the American Psychoanalytic Association, 51S*: 89–98.

Grotstein, J. S. (1978). Inner space: Its dimensions and its coordinates. *The International Journal of Psychoanalysis, 59*: 55–61.

Gruppe, O. (1906a). *Griechische Mythologie und Religionsgeschichte. Band 1.* Munich: Beck, 2013.

Gruppe, O. (1906b). *Griechische Mythologie und Religionsgeschichte. Band 2.* Munich: Beck.

Hadas, M. (1950). *A History of Greek Literature*. New York, NY: Columbia University Press.

Halter, Th. (1998). *König Oedipus. Von Sophokles bis Cocteau*. Stuttgart: Franz Steiner.

Hartmann, H. (1955). Notes on the theory of sublimation. *The Psychoanalytic Study of the Child, 10*: 9–29.

Hartocollis, P. (2005). Origins and evolution of the Oedipus complex as conceptualized by Freud. *The Psychoanalytic Review, 92*: 315–334.

Haynal, A. (1988). *The Technique at Issue. Controversies in Psychoanalysis: From Freud and Ferenczi to Michael Balint*. London: Karnac.

Heiman, N. (1962). Oedipus at Colonus: A study of old age and death. *American Imago, 19*: 91–98.

Horkheimer, M., & Adorno Th. W. (1944). *Dialectic of Enlightenment* (Translation: E. Jephcott). Stanford, CA: Stanford University Press, 2002.

Hornstra, L. (1966). The antecedents of the negative Oedipus complex. *The International Journal of Psychoanalysis, 47*: 531–538.

Jones, E. (1953). *The Life and Work of Sigmund Freud (Volume 1)*. New York, NY: Basic Books.

Jones, E. (1955). *The Life and Work of Sigmund Freud, (Volume 2)*. New York, NY: Basic Books.

Jones, E. (1957). *The Life and Work of Sigmund Freud, (Volume 3)*. New York, NY: Basic Books.

Jones, J. (1976). Art between magic and revolution. *The Psychoanalytic Review, 63*: 427–450.

Joseph, B. (1988). Object relations in clinical practice. *The Psychoanalytic Quarterly, 57*: 626–64.

Kanzer, M. (1948). The ›passing of the Oedipus complex‹ in Greek drama. *The International Journal of Psychoanalysis, 29*: 131–134.

Kanzer, M. (1950). The Oedipus trilogy. *The Psychoanalytic Quarterly, 19*: 561–572.

Kanzer, M. (1964). On interpreting the Oedipus plays. *The Psychoanalytic Study of Society, 3*: 26–38.

Kerènyi, K. (1959). *The Heroes of the Greeks*. London: Thames and Hudson.

Klein, M. (1945). The Oedipus complex in the light of early anxieties. *The International Journal of Psychoanalysis, 26*: 11–33.

Kouretas, D. Th. (1975). *Psychoanalysis—Psychiatriki—Nevrologhia. [Psychoanalysis—Psychiatry—Neurology]*. Athens: Scientific editions GK Parisianos.

Kramer, R. (1995). "The 'bad mother' Freud has never seen": Otto Rank and the birth of object-relations theory. *The Journal of the American Academy of Psychoanalysis, 23*: 293–321.

Krausz, R. (1994). The invisible woman. *The International Journal of Psychoanalysis, 75*: 59–72.

Krüll, M. (1979). *Freud und sein Vater*. Munich: Beck.

Kupfersmid, J. (1992). The "defense" of Sigmund Freud. *Psychotherapy, 29*: 297–309.

Kupfersmid, J. (1993). Freud's rationale for abandoning the seduction theory. *Psychoanalytic Psychology, 10*: 275–290.

Laine, A. (2007). On the edge: The psychoanalyst's transference. *The International Journal of Psychoanalysis, 88*: 1171–1183.

Lampl, A. W., & Oliver, G. W. (1985). Vision without sight. *The Journal of Analytical Psychology, 30*: 297–309.

Laplanche, J. (1986). Von der eingeschränkten zur allgemeinen Verführungstheorie. In: J. Laplanche *Die allgemeine Verführungstheorie und andere Aufsätze* (pp. 199–233). Tübingen: edition discord, 1988.

Lax, R. F. (1995). Motives and determinants of girls' penis envy in the negative oedipal phase. *Journal of Clinical Psychoanalysis, 4*: 297–314.

Lax, R. F. (2007). Father's seduction of daughter entices her into the oedipal phase: Mother's role in the formation of the girl's superego. *Psychoanalytic Psychology, 24*: 306–316.

Lebovici, S. (1982). The origins and development of the Oedipus complex. *The International Journal of Psychoanalysis, 63*: 201–215.

Lederer, W. (1964). Oedipus and the serpent. *The Psychoanalytic Review, 51D*: 79–104.

Lederer, W. (1967). Historical consequences of father-son hostility. *The Psychoanalytic Review, 54B*: 52–80.

Lévi-Strauss, C. (1973). *Anthropologie structurale deux*. Paris: Plon.

Licht, H. (1912). *Sexual Life in ancient Greece*. London: Routledge & Kegan, 1949.

Lichtenstein, H. (1961). Identity and sexuality—A study of their interrelationship in man. *Journal of the American Psychoanalytic Association, 9*: 179–260.

Lidz, Th. (1988). The riddle of the riddle of the Sphinx. *The Psychoanalytic Review, 75*: 35–49.

Loewald, H. W. (1978). Instinct theory, object relations, psychic-structure formation. *Journal of the American Psychoanalytic Association, 26*: 493–506.

Loewald, H. W. (1979). The waning of the Oedipus complex. *Journal of the American Psychoanalytic Association, 27*: 751–775.

Lorand, S. (1939). Contribution to the problem of vaginal orgasm. *The International Journal of Psychoanalysis, 20*: 432–438.

Lorenz, E. (1916). Ödipus auf Kolonos. *Imago 4*: 22–40.

Makari, G. J. (1994). In the eye of the beholder: Helmholtzian perception and the origins of Freud's 1900 theory of transference. *Journal of the American Psychoanalytic Association, 42*: 549–580.

Malinowski, B. (1927). *Sex and Repression in Savage Society*. New York, NY: Meridian Books, 1955.

Mann, D. (1993). The shadow over Oedipus: the father's rivalry with his son. *Free Associations, 4A*: 44–62.

Masson, J. M. (1984). *The Assault on Truth. Freud's Suppression of the Seduction Theory.* New York, NY: Farrar, Straus, & Giroux.

May, R. (1960). *Symbolism in Religion and Literature.* New York, NY: Braziller.

Meehl, P. E. (1994). Subjectivity in psychoanalytic inference: The nagging persistence of Wilhelm Fliess's Achensee question. *Psychoanalysis and Contemporary Thought, 17*: 3–82.

Michels, R. (1986). Oedipus and insight. *The Psychoanalytic Quarterly, 55*: 599–617.

Miller, P. L. (2006). Oedipus Rex revisited. *Modern Psychoanalysis, 31*: 229–250.

Mitchell, J. (1982). Introduction I. In: J. Mitchell & J. Rose (Eds.) *Feminine Sexuality: Jacques Lacan and the École Freudienne* (pp. 1–26). New York, NY: Norton.

Money-Kyrle, R. (1939). *Superstition and Society.* London: Hogarth.

Moore, B. E., & Fine, B. D. (Eds.) (1990). *Psychoanalytic Terms and Concepts.* New Haven, CT: American Psychoanalytic Association.

Moulton, R. (1970). A survey and reevaluation of the concept of penis envy. *Contemporary Psychoanalysis, 7*: 84–104.

Naiman, J. (1992). Freud's Jocasta and Sophocles' Jocasta: Clinical implications of the difference. *The International Journal of Psychoanalysis, 73*: 95–101.

Nauck, A. (1889). *Tragicorum Graecorum Fragments.* Leipzig: Teubner.

Neubauer, P. B. (1960). The one-parent child and his oedipal development. *The Psychoanalytic Study of the Child, 15*: 286–309.

Nunberg, H., & Federn, E. (Eds.) (1974). *Minutes of the Vienna Psychoanalytic Society 1910–1911 (Volume III).* New York, NY: International Universities Press.

Nunberg, H., & Federn, E. (Eds.) (1975). *Minutes of the Vienna Psychoanalytic Society 1912–1916 (Volume IV).* New York, NY: International Universities Press.

Parin, P. In: E. Ticho & W. S. Robbins (1977). Varieties of oedipal distortions in severe character pathologies. *Journal of the American Psychoanalytic Association, 25*: 201–218.

Parsons, M. (1990). Self-knowledge refused and accepted: a psychoanalytic perspective on the ›Bacchae‹ and the ›Oedipus at Colonus‹. *The Journal of Analytical Psychology, 35*: 19–40.

Paul, R. A. (1996). *Moses and Civilizations: The Meaning behind Freud's Myth.* New Haven, CT: Yale University Press.

Pilikian, H. I. (1974). Interview with D. Keay. *Guardian Newspaper 17 July 1974* [cited in Steiner, J. (1985). Turning a blind eye: The cover up for Oedipus. *The International Review of Psycho-Analysis, 12*: 161–172].

Politzer, H. (1972). Ödipus auf Kolonos: Versuch über eine Gemeinsamkeit von Psychoanalyse und Literaturkritik. *Psyche—Zeitschrift für Psychoanalyse und ihre Anwendungen, 26*: 489–519.

Pollock, G. H. (1986). Oedipus examined and reconsidered: The myth, the developmental stage, the universal theme, the conflict, and the complex. *The Annual of Psychoanalysis, 14*: 77–106.

Preller, L. (1875). *Griechische Mythologie (Band 2)*. Berlin: Weidmannsche Buchhandlung.

Preller, L. (1921). *Griechische Mythologie (Band 3)*. Berlin: Weidmannsche Buchhandlung, erneuert von C. Robert.

Priel, B. (2002). Who killed Laius?: On Sophocles' enigmatic message. *The International Journal of Psychoanalysis, 83*: 433–443.

Rachman, A. W. (1997). The suppression and censorship of Ferenczi's confusion of tongues paper. *Psychoanalytic Inquiry, 17*: 459–485.

Rado, Ch. (1956). "Oedipus The King": An interpretation. *The Psychoanalytic Review, 43*: 228–234.

Rado, Ch. (1962). Oedipus at Colonus an interpretation. *American Imago, 19*: 235–242.

Rank, O. (1913). Mythologie und Psychoanalyse. In: O. Rank *Psychoanalytische Beiträge zur Mythenforschung* (pp. 1–20). Hamburg: Severus, 2010.

Rank, O. (1926). *The Incest Theme in Literature and Legend*. Baltimore: John Hopkins University Press, 1992.

Raphael-Leff, J. (1990). If Oedipus was an Egyptian. *The International Review of Psycho-Analysis, 17*: 309–335.

Rascovsky, A., & Rascovsky, M. (1972). The prohibition of incest, filicide and the sociocultural process. *The International Journal of Psychoanalysis, 53*: 271–276.

Rascovsky, M. (1968). On the genesis of acting out and psychopathic behaviour in Sophocles' Oedipus—notes on filicide. *The International Journal of Psychoanalysis, 49*: 390–394.

Reed, G. S. (2008). Turning heads: A commentary on ›A man who was tied up‹. *The International Journal of Psychoanalysis, 89*: 497–501.

Reich, W. (1932). *The Invasion of Compulsory Sex-Morality*. New York, NY: Farrar, Straus, & Giroux, 1971.

Reik, Th. (1920). Oedipus and the Sphinx. In: G. H. Pollock & J. M. Ross (Eds.). *The Oedipus Papers* (pp. 21–65). Madison, CT: International Universities Press, 1988.

Riklin, F., & White, W. A. (1915). Wishfulfillment and symbolism in fairy tales. *The Psychoanalytic Review, 2*: 327–340.

Roazen, P. (1976). *Sigmund Freud und sein Kreis*. Gießen: Psychosozial, 1997.

Robert, C. (1915). *Oidipus—Geschichte eines poetischen Stoffs im griechischen Altertum (Band 1)*. Berlin: Weidmannsche Buchhandlung.

Róheim, G. (1934). *The Riddle of the Sphinx or Human Origins*. New York, NY: Harper and Row, 1974.

Róheim, G. (1946). Teiresias and other seers. *The Psychoanalytic Review, 33*: 314–334.

Róheim, G. (1953). The language of birds. *American Imago, 10*: 3–14.

Roll, S., & Abel, Th. (1988). Variations in secondary themes of the oedipal legend. *The Journal of the American Academy of Psychoanalysis, 16*: 537–547.

Roscher, W. H. (Ed.) (1884–1890). *Ausführliches Lexikon der griechischen und römischen Mythologie (Erster Band)*. Leipzig: Teubner.

Roscher, W. H. (Ed.) (1897–1909). *Ausführliches Lexikon der griechischen und römischen Mythologie (Dritter Band)*. Leipzig: Teubner.

Roscher, W. H. (Ed.) (1909–1915). *Ausführliches Lexikon der griechischen und römischen Mythologie (Vierter Band)*. Leipzig: Teubner.

Rosenman, S. (1982). The legend of Oedipus: Victimizing implantations. *American Imago, 39*: 119–132.

Ross, J. M. (1982). Oedipus revisited—Laius and the "Laius complex". *The Psychoanalytic Study of the Child, 37*: 169–200.

Ross, J. M. (1984). The darker side of fatherhood: clinical and developmental ramifications of the "Laius motif". In: G. M. Pollock & J. M. Ross (Eds.) *The Oedipus Papers* (pp. 389–417). Madison, CT: International Universities Press, 1988.

Rudnytsky, P. L. (1987). *Freud and Oedipus*. New York, NY: Columbia University Press.

Rudnytsky, P. L. (1999). Wrecking crews. *American Imago, 56*: 285–298.

Rusbridger, R. (2004). Elements of the Oedipus complex: A Kleinian account. *The International Journal of Psychoanalysis, 85*: 731–747.

Sadger, J. (1910). *Heinrich von Kleist. Eine pathographisch-psychologische Studie*. Wiesbaden: Bergmann.

Sadow, L., Gedo, J. E., Miller, J. A., Pollock, G. H., Sabshin, M., & Schlesinger, N. (1976). The process of hypothesis change in three early psychoanalytic concepts. *Psychological Issues Monograph, 34/35*: 255–353.

Sandler, J., & Freud, A. (1983). Discussions in the Hampstead index of the ego and the mechanisms of defense. *Journal of the American Psychoanalytic Association, 31S*: 19–146.

Sapisochin, G. (1999). "My heart belongs to daddy": Some reflections on the difference between generations as the organiser of the triangular structure of the mind. *The International Journal of Psychoanalysis, 80*: 755–767.

Schiller, F. (1789). *The Death of Wallenstein*. Free Ebook #6787. Project Gutenberg, 2006

Schimek, J. G. (1975). The interpretations of the past: Childhood trauma, psychical reality, and historical truth. *Journal of the American Psychoanalytic Association, 23*: 845–865.

Schimek, J. G. (1987). Fact and fantasy in the seduction theory: A historical review. *Journal of the American Psychoanalytic Association, 35*: 937–964.

Schmidt, B. (1877). *Griechische Märchen, Sagen und Volkslieder. Gesammelt, übersetzt, und erläutert.* Leipzig: Teubner.

Schneiderhan, F. W. (1852). *Die Sage vom Ödipus.* Göttingen: Dieterichsche Buchhandlung.

Schur, M. (1972). *Freud: Living and Dying.* New York, NY: International Universities Press.

Seidenberg, R., & Papathomopoulos, E. (1960). Oedipus at Colonus and the aged Sophocles. *The Psychoanalytic Quarterly, 29*: 236–239.

Seidenberg, R., & Papathomopoulos, E. (1962). Daughters who tend their fathers, a literary survey. *The Psychoanalytic Study of Society, 2*: 135–160.

Shengold, L. (1963). The parent as Sphinx. *Journal of the American Psychoanalytic Association, 11*: 725–751.

Simon, B. (1992). "Incest—See under Oedipus complex": The history of an error in psychoanalysis. *Journal of the American Psychoanalytic Association, 40*: 955–988.

Simonsuuri, K. (1997). Editorial: The secret code. *International Forum of Psychoanalysis, 6*: 1–3.

Sophocles. (1889). *The Oedipus at Colonus* (Jepp, R. translator). Cambridge: Cambridge University Press. [www.perseus.tufts.edu/ hoper/text?doc=Perseus%3Atext%3A1999.01.0190%3Acard%3D1 last accessed 21 April 2016].

Sophocles. (1991a). *Oedipus the King* (Grene, D. translator). In: D. Grene & R. Lattimore (Eds.) *Sophocles I* (pp. 9–76). Chicago, IL: University of Chicago Press.

Sophocles. (1991b). *Antigone* (Grene, D., translator). In: D. Grene & R. Lattimore (Eds.) *Sophocles I* (pp. 159–212). Chicago, IL: University of Chicago Press.

Sophocles. (2010). *ΟΙΔΙΠΟΥΣ ΤΥΡΑΝΝΟΣ.* [http://ps.privateschools.gr/ lykeio/b_lyk/Arxaia_Elliniki_Glossa_Genikis_Paideias/Sofokleoys_ Oidipoys_Tyrranos_Aias.pdf last accessed 4 May 2016].

Squire, C. (1975). *Celtic Myth and Legend.* Newcastle: Newcastle Publishing.

Steiner, J. (1990). The retreat from truth to omnipotence in Sophocles' Oedipus at Colonus. *The International Review of Psycho-Analysis, 17*: 227–237.

Steiner, J. (1994). In Vienna veritas …. *The International Journal of Psychoanalysis, 75*: 511–573.

St. Clair, M. (1961). A note on the guilt of Oedipus. *The Psychoanalytic Review, 48A*: 111–114.

Stewart, H. (1961). Jocasta's crimes. *The International Journal of Psychoanalysis, 42*: 424–430.

Stimmel, B. (2004). The cause is worse: Remeeting Jocasta. *The International Journal of Psychoanalysis, 85*: 1175–1189.

Stoller, R. J. (1985). *Presentations of Gender*. New Haven, CT: Yale University Press.

Sylwan, B. (1984). An untoward event: Ou la guerre du trauma de Breuer à Freud de Jones à Ferenczi. *Cahiers Confrontation 2*: 101–115.

Thass-Thienemann, Th. (1957). Oedipus and the Sphinx: The linguistic approach to unconscious fantasies. *The Psychoanalytic Review, 44*: 10–33.

Vaillant, G. E. (1992). The historical origins and future potential of Sigmund Freud's concept of the mechanisms of defence. *The International Review of Psycho-Analysis, 19*: 36–50.

Van der Sterren, D. (1974). *Ödipus. Nach den Tragödien des Sophokles. Eine psychoanalytische Studie*. Frankfurt/M: Fischer, 1986.

Van der Sterren, H. A. (1952). The "King Oedipus" of Sophocles. *The International Journal of Psychoanalysis, 33*: 343–350.

Waelder, R. (1963). *Basic Theory of Psychoanalysis*. New York, NY: Schocken, 1971.

Wallace, E. R. (1983). *Freud and Anthropology. A History and Reappraisal*. Psychological Issues Monograph, 55. New York, NY: International Universities Press.

Werman, D. (1979). Methodological problems in the psychoanalytic interpretation of literature: A review of studies of Sophocles' Antigone. *Journal of the American Psychoanalytic Association, 27*: 451–478.

Whitebook, J. (1995). Athene und McKenna. Zur Integration klassischer und neuerer psychoanalytischer Theorie. *Psyche—Zeitschrift für Psychoanalyse und ihre Anwendungen, 49*: 207–226.

Wirth, H. (2007). Schismatic processes in the psychoanalytic movement and their impact on the formation of theories. *International Forum of Psychoanalysis, 16*: 4–11.

Yerushalmi, Y. H. (1989). Freud on the "Historical Novel": From the manuscript draft (1934) of Moses and monotheism. *The International Journal of Psychoanalysis, 70*: 375–394.

Young, R. M. (1988). Consider Laius. *Free Associations, 1N*: 150.

Zepf, S., & Zepf, F. D. (2008). Trauma and traumatic neurosis—Freud's concepts revisited. *The International Journal of Psychoanalysis, 89*: 331–353.

INDEX